HOUSMAN'S

Land of Lost Content

That is the land of lost content,

I see it shining plain,

The happy highways where I went

And cannot come again.

HOUSMAN'S

Land of Lost Content

A CRITICAL STUDY OF

A Shropshire Lad

BY B. J. LEGGETT

•

THE UNIVERSITY OF TENNESSEE PRESS

KNOXVILLE

LIBRARY OF CONGRESS CATALOG CARD NUMBER 71–100407

STANDARD BOOK NUMBER 87049–106–7

COPYRIGHT © 1970 BY THE UNIVERSITY OF

TENNESSEE PRESS.   ALL RIGHTS RESERVED.

MANUFACTURED IN THE UNITED STATES OF AMERICA.

FIRST EDITION.

FOR CORINNE

CONTENTS

PREFACE

A *Shropshire Lad* contains the great majority of A. E. Housman's poems which are still of interest to twentieth-century readers. Thus, a reassessment of this work, upon which his recognition as a poet is based, constitutes a reappraisal of Housman's art as well. I am aware that some of my contentions about the nature of *A Shropshire Lad* and Housman's art in general are contrary to those in acceptance today, and that some readers, well versed in the traditional view of Housman, may be reluctant to pursue my thesis that *A Shropshire Lad* is unified thematically and structurally. However, even those who hold to the accepted view of Housman may find some value in the discussions of the individual lyrics, for at present there is no critical work which offers a systematic examination of Housman's poetry.

The primary concern of this book is with the structural and thematic unity of *A Shropshire Lad*. It attempts to demonstrate that Housman's poetry may be read apart from biographical reference and personal belief, and, more specifically, that *A Shropshire Lad,* which is central to an understanding of Housman, is a self-contained and unified work of art. The greater part of the study is devoted to structural problems, both of the individual lyrics and of the work as a whole. However, it is impossible to avoid discussion of the thematic continuity upon which the structure rests, and of related critical problems which have escaped the scrutiny of previous criticism.

The chapters that follow constitute an attempt to shift the direction of Housman criticism from questions of personality and belief toward an examination of the art of his poetry. They are based on the assumption that if he is to be understood he must be studied as a poet, through a systematic and detailed analysis of his best-known and most highly regarded work. This study also calls into question the dominant view of his poetry that has been most responsible for the dilemma of Housman criticism—the notion that his verses present a simplicity that eludes analysis. On the contrary, the need for close critical examination is made evident by even a cursory review of available criticism.

It may appear that restricting this study to *A Shropshire Lad* unduly limits any analysis of Housman's poetry, but special reasons exist for such a restriction. In the first place, *A Shropshire Lad* contains the majority of the poems Housman published in his lifetime. The only other volume of verse he assembled, *Last Poems*, was issued twenty-six years after *A Shropshire Lad*. The other collections, *More Poems* and *Additional Poems*, salvaged from the notebooks and published after his death by his brother Laurence, represent verse Housman elected not to publish himself. *A Shropshire Lad* thus constitutes the core of Housman's work. It is upon this volume of poems that his reputation must ultimately rest. The posthumous poems are generally of an inferior quality,[1] and even *Last Poems* contains a number of verses that, although written at the same time as the poems in *A Shropshire Lad,* were not included in the earlier volume.

Finally, *A Shropshire Lad* is of special interest because of the evidence that Housman may have regarded it as a unified work, not simply as a collection of separate lyrics. It could be conjectured that he excluded some of the poems later published in *Last Poems* because he had some particular arrangement in

---

[1] Stephen Spender's assessment is that "the posthumous poems are interesting but on the whole . . . do him a disservice, because although they contain beautiful lines, and even whole poems as good as any he wrote, they say in a cruder form, which sometimes amounts almost to parody, what he has said before. . . ." Quoted in Grant Richards, *Housman 1897–1936* (New York, 1942), p. 369.

mind. It is certain that the poems are not arranged chronologically, and it is strange that, in filling out his small volume, Housman should pass over many poems that he later published. Moreover, Housman refused to allow *A Shropshire Lad* to be published in one volume with *Last Poems* as a collection, or to allow poems from the earlier book to be included in anthologies, although he did not make the same demand of *Last Poems*. Housman's publisher Grant Richards concludes from these facts: "His idea *may* have been that he looked on the book as a sequence of poems and in consequence disliked any one being divorced from its fellows."[2] None of these bits of evidence is conclusive, but together they support his publisher's view that Housman regarded the arrangement of the sixty-three poems of the volume as significant. The contention of this study is that *A Shropshire Lad* is indeed unified thematically and that careful attention to the ordering of the poems is essential to an understanding of the work.

There has been, of course, much perceptive criticism of Housman's verse, but it is scattered and, on the whole, fragmentary, appearing as short analyses of individual poems or as essays devoted to quite restricted subjects. I am indebted to these critics, even though I have had to reject many of their assumptions. I am particularly indebted to three, whose names appear in the following pages with some frequency. John Stevenson's essays on Housman's pastoral mode and his lyric tradition have reinforced and, in some cases, modified my own views, and I trust I have given proper credit to the influence of his studies, perhaps the most valuable of recent Housman criticism. Nesca A. Robb was the earliest of Housman's commentators to deal with the unity of his poetry, and although her essay has been dismissed by subsequent scholarship, I must acknowledge that I am not the first to have conceived of *A Shropshire Lad* as a unified whole. Furthermore, I find myself in substantial agreement with many of her findings, even though she and I pursued

2 *Ibid.*, p. 53.

different methods in our studies and reached somewhat different conclusions. Finally, I must express my debt to Tom Burns Haber, whose studies of Housman's notebooks and the printer's copy of *A Shropshire Lad* are valuable aids in ascertaining some idea of Housman's method of composition and the ordering of his poems. It will be seen later that Professor Haber and I are at odds on the central question of the structure of *A Shropshire Lad*, but this fact does not lessen my debt to his scholarship.

The preliminary study which led to this book was begun under the direction of Alton Morris, of the University of Florida, and the book was completed with the aid of a grant from the National Foundation for the Arts and the Humanities. I am grateful to Professor Morris for his encouragement and wise counsel and to the foundation for providing the means by which the project could be pursued to its conclusion. I must also express my appreciation to The University of Tennessee Graduate School for providing the summer grant under which the final manuscript revisions were made, and to the editors of the *Explicator* and *English Language Notes* for permission to reprint materials of mine which appeared in slightly different form in these journals. I also wish to thank Colby College Library for permission to quote extensively from *A Shropshire Lad* (Jubilee Edition, with Notes and a Bibliography by Carl J. Weber, Waterville, Maine, 1946).

B. J. Leggett

Knoxville, Tennessee
April, 1970

HOUSMAN'S

Land of Lost Content

INTRODUCTION

*A*ny assessment of A. E. Housman's present stature as a poet must begin with the well-known but curious fact that his poetry, while it has become widely read and even highly regarded in some circles, has failed to give rise to a significant body of criticism. In an age of close reading and analysis, no systematic study of Housman's poetry has been attempted. The commentaries which have been produced are given, on the whole, to discussions of Housman's pessimism or to probings of the personality which seems to lie beneath the surface of his poems. The last decade has witnessed some fragmentary efforts to re-examine his poetic contribution, but it remains essentially true that few critics have become involved with Housman's art. In 1945, Robert W. Stallman's critical bibliography revealed that of the 177 poems in *The Collected Poems of A. E. Housman* only 27 had been analyzed in whole or in part.[1] In 1958, Norman Marlow, in a biography of Housman, found little change, stating that "there is still no comprehensive study of his poetry and very little balanced criticism of it."[2] More than a decade has passed, and the same assessment may be offered with little qualification; yet Housman's reputation has grown appreciably since his death in 1936, as William White has shown in a

1 "Annotated Bibliography of A. E. Housman: A Critical Study," *PMLA*, LX (1945), 463.
2 *A. E. Housman: Scholar and Poet* (Minneapolis, 1958), p. vii.

survey of the increasing use of his poems in anthologies and the frequency of their reissue in collections.[3]

The lack of critical attention paid to a poet of Housman's standing would appear strange indeed were there not compelling reasons for it, not the least of which is the nature of the verse he produced. The notion has persisted that the simplicity and directness of Housman's poetry obviates the necessity for close analysis. A year after the poet's death, Louis Kronenberger found that not much remained to be said about Housman's art: "One could hardly tie him in with anything very original concerning life itself, or explain at great length a philosophy that was almost self-explanatory, or find special meaning in him that the rest of the world has neglected to find."[4] Kronenberger's feeling that the nature of Housman's verse precludes any kind of detailed criticism is obviously shared by later critics. Oliver Robinson issued in 1950 what he called a critical essay on Housman's poetry, but his discussion of the poems amounts to no more than noting certain themes and quoting the lines in which they appear. Significantly, he remarks that "usually the poems are self-explanatory."[5] Certainly no opinion was so predominant among Housman's early commentators as that which asserted that his verses are marked by an essential simplicity of form and thought,[6] and this view is still in evidence today.

While Housman's clarity and directness have been praised widely,[7] the singular nature of his poetry has without question

[3] "A. E. Housman Anthologized: Evidence in the Growth of a Poet's Reputation," *Bulletin of Bibliography*, XXI (1953), 43–48, 68–72.

[4] "A Note on A. E. Housman," *Nation*, CXLV (Dec. 18, 1937), 690.

[5] *Angry Dust: The Poetry of A. E. Housman* (Boston, 1950), p. 22.

[6] See, for example, H. P. Collins, *Modern Poetry* (London, 1925), p. 74; Ian Scott-Kilvert, *A. E. Housman* (London, 1955), p. 26; Louis Untermeyer, *Modern American Poetry; Modern British Poetry* (New York, 1942), II, 102; Herbert Gorman, *The Procession of Masks* (Boston, 1923), p. 171; James Brannin, "Alfred Housman," *Sewanee Review*, XXXIII (1925), 192–94; and Rica Brenner, "Alfred Edward Housman," in *Ten Modern Poets* (New York, 1930), p. 188.

[7] There are exceptions. Edith Sitwell objected that "this admired sim-

retarded any serious attempt at the kind of analysis which has enriched the poetry of many of his contemporaries. Furthermore, the assumption of the critics that a simplicity of form produces a self-explanatory poetry is misleading, if not completely invalid; yet this early view of Housman's verse has not been successfully challenged. If Housman's poetry is indeed self-explanatory, one ought to find substantial agreement on the interpretation of his poems, but this has not been the case. Stallman, who classified the views of Housman's commentators in 1945, found that the critics disagreed on almost every point of Housman criticism.[8]

The truth is that Housman's poetry is more subtle and more complex than has been acknowledged by his commentators. Part of the problem lies in a confusion between the simplicity of the forms which Housman inherited and followed and his own distinctive use of these forms.[9] Both the ballad and the pastoral, the two genres which inform his verse, are marked by a surface simplicity; and it is obvious that the directness of the ballad and the ironic naïveté of the pastoral control the tone of his poetry. But only rarely have critics looked beneath the smooth surface of his poems to glimpse the perplexities of his themes and structures.

What has concerned Housman's critics since the publication of *A Shropshire Lad* in 1896 is the enigma of Housman the man as it is reflected in his verse. He has suffered, like Byron, from the fact that his personality is of more interest to many readers than his poetry, and that for some scholars the poetry

plicity of his seems not so much the result of passion finding its expression in an inevitable phrase . . . as the result of a bare and threadbare texture" ("Three Eras of Modern Poetry," in *Trio* by Osbert, Edith, and Sacheverell Sitwell [London, 1938], p. 104). Other critics have described Housman's style as "threadbare"; for example, Conrad Aiken in *New Republic*, LXXXIX (Nov. 11, 1936), 51–52, and Edwin Muir in *London Mercury*, XXXV (1936), 63.

8 Stallman, p. 480.

9 See Elisabeth Schneider, *Aesthetic Motive* (New York, 1939), for a discussion of this problem with special reference to Housman.

is valuable only as a key to the personality. It must be admitted that the portrait of the man emerging from the biographies encourages such a concern, for Housman's life produced a series of minor crises which scholars have attempted to relate to the tragic view of life which permeates his poetry. The death of Housman's mother on his twelfth birthday, his sister Katherine Symons reports, had such a lasting effect on him that death became an obsession.[10] His failure in the Greats examinations at Oxford disgraced him in the eyes of his family and caused him to seek refuge in London for a time as a civil servant. The death of his father in 1894 not only constituted a personal loss but also threw him into extreme financial difficulties. Finally, his relationship with Moses Jackson, a fellow student at Oxford, was the source of deep emotional scars, climaxed in 1887 by Jackson's departure for India after the friendship was strained, some scholars infer, by an unnatural attachment on Housman's part.[11]

But Housman's personality would perhaps not have attracted so much critical attention were it not, again, for the nature of his poetry. The formal and metrical simplicity of Housman's lyrics has directed interest away from the poetry itself, toward the personality which seems to be revealed. It is a poetry, says Stephen Spender, which seems to hide "some nagging Housmanish secret."[12] Spender is intrigued, as are a number of other critics, by the autobiographical tone of the poems and the suggestion that personal tragedy is concealed in the poetry.[13] This sense of personal tragedy is no doubt prompted by the lads of Shropshire who are obsessed with death even in the

10 *Alfred Edward Housman: Recollections,* by Katherine E. Symons, et al. (New York, 1937) , p. 8.

11 The biographies by both George Watson (*A. E. Housman: A Divided Life* [London, 1957]) and Maude M. Hawkins (*A. E. Housman: Man Behind a Mask* [Chicago, 1958]) propose the theory that Housman was homosexually attracted to Jackson.

12 "The Essential Housman," in *The Making of a Poem* (London, 1955) , p. 159.

13 *Ibid.,* p. 162.

prime of life, who grieve for departed friends and express a
sense of guilt for nameless sins. The assumption that such an
obsession with guilt and death must have its basis in some
deep-seated psychological disorder has consequently led to the
notion that Housman's poetry is merely the embodiment of his
personal dilemma. It has also been responsible for the widely
held dictum that Housman's personality must be seen as the
key to his poetry and the resulting corollary that the poetry
may contain the key to his personality.[14]

It is obvious that such an approach, although interesting
and perhaps ultimately valuable in an understanding of the
genesis of creativity, dangerously undermines any effort to consider Housman's poetry on its own merits, apart from biographical considerations. John K. Ryan illustrates the problems
involved when he insists on "intimate sources" for Housman's
poetry and suggests that Housman, as a poet, presents a special
problem which cannot be solved by conventional methods.[15]
Other examples of this attitude, which came into prominence
before Housman's death, are widespread. Ultimately, it led to
the critical position that the poems, as transmutations of the
poet's experience, could not be explained until he revealed
the clue.[16]

Housman, of course, revealed no such clue. In fact, he repeatedly denied that one existed. In a letter to a French student who had inquired about the personal basis of his poetry
he replied, "The Shropshire Lad is an imaginary figure, with
something of my temperament and view of life. Very little in

[14] George Watson stated in his biography of Housman: "In this study . . .
his poetry becomes the indispensable key to a personality which even those
who knew him best always confessed to finding adamantine" (p. 11).

[15] "Defeatist as Poet," *Catholic World*, CXLI (1935), 35.

[16] See Rica Brenner, p. 191. For further examples of this view see J. P.
Bishop, "The Poetry of A. E. Housman," *Poetry*, LVI (1940), 150; Lawrence
Leighton, "One View of Housman," *Poetry*, LII (1938), 95; H. W. Garrod,
"Housman: 1939," *Essays and Studies*, XXV (1939), 7–21; and A. F. Allison,
"The Poetry of A. E. Housman," *Review of English Studies*, XIX (1943),
279.

the book is biographical."[17] He further said, in regard to some supposed crisis that had produced his pessimistic philosophy:

> I have never had any such thing as a "crisis of pessimism." In the first place, I am not a pessimist but a "pejorist" (as George Eliot said she was not an optimist but a meliorist) ; and that is owing to my observation of the world, not to personal circumstances. Secondly, I did not begin to write poetry in earnest until the really emotional part of my life was over; and my poetry, as far as I could make out, sprang chiefly from physical conditions, such as a relaxed sore throat during my most prolific period, the first five months of 1895.[18]

This statement is supported by another, solicited by Wilfrid Scawen Blunt, who wrote in *My Diaries* of a conversation with Housman in which he asked the poet whether there was any episode in his life which suggested the gruesome character of his poems. "Housman assured me it was not so. He had lived as a boy in Worcestershire, not in Shropshire, though within sight of the Shropshire hills, and there was nothing gruesome to record."[19]

Here perhaps the matter should have rested, but the "nagging Housmanish secret" of the poetry has continued to overshadow the poet's own statements. Doubtless Housman, like all poets, relied heavily on his personal experiences and emotions to provide the materials for his art. Yet to insist that his poetry can be understood only in a biographical context, the position of the early commentators, is to limit unnecessarily the range of criticism and to subordinate the poetry to the poet. At its furthest extreme, this approach finds worth in the poetry only as it explains the character of the poet, and the biographical critics thus turn Housman into a psychological case study.[20]

[17] Quoted in Marlow, p. 150.
[18] *Ibid.*
[19] Quoted in Richards, pp. 105–106.
[20] Benjamin Brooks, for example, has stated that the "poetic reasons" for accepting Housman died away with the Georgians, and it is only personal

Their tendency is to make use of the poetry only as a guide to the poet, and the result is a failure to interpret Housman's poetry as poetry. Furthermore, although a great part of existing Housman criticism is based on biographical conjecture, no significant results are evident. Housman continues to be read and studied for irrelevant reasons, and his critical standing has no doubt been damaged as a consequence.

Housman's reputation has been further injured by a similar tendency to regard his poetry as philosophy. Because he chose to consider in his poems some of the great commonplaces of life—the transience of human existence, the fear of oblivion in death, the injustice of man's condition on earth—he was early labeled a "message" poet, more specifically a pessimist, and his poetry has been dismissed frequently on these grounds. The preoccupation with the philosophical import of Housman's works has taken several forms, but the weight of opinion is that his philosophical beliefs, being unsound, prevent the appreciation or enjoyment of his poetry.[21] In short, many commentators have pronounced Housman a philosophical poet only to reject his poetry because they found his philosophy to be perverse or inconsequential. Cleanth Brooks concludes that Housman is not even the perfect minor poet, for he "had no . . . world view to set up. Intellectually, he has not moved far past an austere scepticism."[22] The other charge which has been leveled frequently against Housman's thought is its apparent

and psychological reasons which make him of interest today ("A. E. Housman's Collected Poetry," *Nineteenth Century*, CXXVIII [1940], 71). Ernest Moss, who finds in Housman "a longing for return to the elemental womb," concludes that "it is improbable that the mass of his work can be enjoyed as poetry" (quoted in Stallman, p. 484).

21 See Stallman's critical bibliography of Housman for a classification of the conflicting views on Housman's philosophy.

22 "The Whole of Housman," *Kenyon Review*, III (1941), 105–106. R. P. Blackmur concurs that Housman "was not a great minor poet"; he was not a profound thinker but "a desperately solemn purveyor of a single adolescent emotion" (*The Expense of Greatness* [Gloucester, Mass., 1958], pp. 202, 204). Even Louis MacNeice, who is generally sympathetic to Housman, holds that although Housman's philosophy is essential to his poetry, it has

inconsistency—the poems have no standard of value and are thus at odds with each other, Housman answers the philosophical questions he raises in contradictory ways, and his beliefs baffle the reader and fail to advance his understanding.[23]

These would be valid objections if Housman's achievement were philosophic rather than aesthetic. If, as John K. Ryan said of Housman, "the appeal and power of the philosophical poet must ultimately rest on his thoughts rather than on the way he expresses them,"[24] then Housman may easily be dismissed, for he obviously failed to advance any kind of sound philosophical system. But such an approach has serious drawbacks. No harm is done in speaking on the colloquial level of the "philosophy" of a poet, but to apply the criteria of philosophy to poetry may lead to confusion. For example, to say that a philosophical statement is contradictory is to discredit it. Yet Cleanth Brooks, who objects to Housman on philosophical grounds, has devoted an entire volume to showing that "paradox is the language appropriate and inevitable to poetry. It is the scientist whose truth requires a language purged of every trace of paradox. . . ."[25] Again, clarity and specificity are virtues of the language of philosophy, but modern criticism has held that one characteristic of good poetry is ambiguity, the ability of a poetic statement to convey two or more sometimes conflicting meanings simultaneously. One could continue such a distinction almost indefinitely, but it should be clear that poetry is not philosophy, and a confusion between the two is always injurious to the poet. It is to be doubted that Housman's poetry can be understood sufficiently if it is seen only as a set of truths to be accepted or denied.

---

very little meaning ("Housman in Retrospect," *New Republic,* CII [1940], 583).

[23] These three views, respectively, were advanced by Jacob Bronowski (p. 221), Hugh Molson ("The Philosophies of Hardy and Housman," *Quarterly Review,* CCLXVIII [1937], 207–208), and Lawrence Leighton (p. 98).

[24] Ryan, p. 34.

[25] *The Well Wrought Urn* (New York, 1947), p. 3.

His poetry cannot be explained by reference to a philosophical system or a set of beliefs. Any attempt to do so violates the distinctive nature of poetry and ignores the valuable lessons of much modern criticism. It also ignores Housman's own aesthetic principles, which he advanced in the Leslie Stephen Lecture for 1933, entitled *The Name and Nature of Poetry*. Here Housman stated clearly and unmistakably that, for him, poetry was not thought, but emotion. He said: "I think that to transfuse emotion—not to transmit thought but to set up in the reader's sense a vibration corresponding to what was felt by the writer—is the peculiar function of poetry." The essence of poetry for Housman is not the abstracted thought but its expression: "Poetry is not the thing said but a way of saying it." He even denies that poetry is a product of the intellect: "Meaning is of the intellect, poetry is not . . . the intellect is not the fount of poetry . . . it may actually hinder its production."[26]

What is more, men who knew Housman well have attested to the fact that he was not interested in philosophy. Canon J. T. Nance, who was a tutor in St. John's College, Oxford, when Housman was a scholar there, has written: ". . . Housman did not take any interest in Greek philosophy. His interests were in pure scholarship."[27] Percy Withers reports that once when he attempted to discuss with Housman some questions in metaphysics, Housman replied angrily, "That is a subject I will not discuss." Withers thus concludes that Housman objected to "the whole realm of philosophic thought."[28] It is strange then, in view of so much evidence of his hostility to philosophical analysis and abstraction, that Housman should be regarded by many as a poet of thought, for the essence of his poetry lies, in his own words, not in the thing said, but in a way of saying it.

[26] *A. E. Housman: Selected Prose*, ed. by John Carter (New York, 1961), pp. 172, 187–88.
[27] Quoted in Richards, p. 322.
[28] *Ibid.*, pp. 57–58.

II

THEME: THE PROBLEM OF CHANGE

*N*orthrop Frye has observed that the story of both the loss and the regaining of identity is the framework of all literature.[1] Whether one would wish to subscribe to such an encyclopedic view of art, it is nevertheless true that the most primitive element of Frye's story, the loss of a world of innocence and permanence and the discovery of an alien world of change and death, is a central one in our culture as well as our literature. In this and the chapter which follows I wish to examine *A Shropshire Lad* in terms of such an informing theme. It may be stated briefly in two different but related ways. In the simplest terms, the theme which underlies the sixty-three lyrics of the work represents a concern with the problem of change, the transience which characterizes existence, and a search for some kind of permanence in the midst of change. In mythic terms, it is the theme of innocence and experience—the transition from a view of life which sees an identity with the external world to one which is characterized by a feeling of alienation, a sense of being separated from the world. It is important to recognize, however, that these two statements are no more than two perspectives of the same theme. Since the loss of innocence occurs with the awareness that existence is not unchanging, but is instead subject to the

---

1 *The Educated Imagination* (Bloomington, 1964), p. 55. My formulation of the archetype of innocence and experience is based partly on Frye's distinctions here and in the essay "Archetypal Criticism: Theory of Myths" in *Anatomy of Criticism* (Princeton, 1957).

forces of mutability and death, permanence may be equated with innocence, change with experience. This conception is, of course, an elementary one in twentieth-century criticism, yet it is crucial to an understanding of the thematic and structural unity of *A Shropshire Lad*.

John Stevenson has stated bluntly that "the whole theme of Housman's poetry . . . is the loss of innocence."[2] He finds that the theme is most often manifested in the Shropshire lad himself: "The conflict that becomes dramatized in the action, and in his own mind, is the conflict between the actual and the ideal, the world of being and the world of becoming; what Mr. Cleanth Brooks has described as 'the world of "Presences" that are absolute and do not change, and the world of becoming which passes from birth to decay and death.' "[3] What the lad discovers is what the innocent inevitably discovers after the fall: the world which was once a part of himself is now an alien world of endless change in which the only certainty is, ironically, the thing most alien, death.

This is the world which *A Shropshire Lad* depicts. It is, of course, not located geographically but in the emotions and in the imagination. Its tone is that of the pastoral elegy,[4] characterized by the mask of naïveté, the setting of the uncomplicated country life, the longing for a return to the simple in the face of the increasing complexity of the problems of life and death. It is manifested from the very beginning of *A Shropshire Lad* by an obsession with the essential transience of the human situation. The opening poem, "1887," in fact, as its title suggests, serves to juxtapose the mood of the work against the more prevailing optimism of its historical setting. *A Shropshire Lad* begins, ironically, with the spirit of celebration and faith in the permanence and stability of the British crown which

2 "The Martyr as Innocent: Housman's Lonely Lad," *South Atlantic Quarterly*, LVII (1958), 70.

3 *Ibid.*, p. 77.

4 See Michael Macklem, "The Elegiac Theme in Housman," *Queen's Quarterly*, LIX (1952), 39–52.

characterized Victoria's Golden Jubilee. "1887" opens with a description of the fires which dot the English hillside in honor of the fiftieth year of Victoria's reign:

> From Clee to heaven the beacon burns,
>   The shires have seen it plain,
> From north and south the sign returns
>   And beacons burn again.
>
> Look left, look right, the hills are bright,
>   The dales are light between,
> Because 'tis fifty years to-night
>   That God has saved the Queen.
>   (ll. 1–8)

This last line, twice paraphrased in the poem, underlines the spiritual basis on which the crown, at least traditionally, rests in the English view. But the whole point of "1887" is that the permanence of the crown is based on the expendability of its subjects, as demonstrated by the emphasis on the British soldier, who in the work of saving the Queen, "shared the work with God" (l. 12). The soldiers in the poem become "saviours," and in its use of Christian symbols "1887" replaces the spiritual basis for the salvation of the crown with a purely physical one. Stanza 4 speaks of the soldiers in words traditionally associated with Christ:

> To skies that knit their heartstrings right,
>   To fields that bred them brave,
> The saviours come not home to-night:
>   Themselves they could not save.
>   (ll. 13–16)

The last line suggests Matthew 27:42, where the chief priests, scribes, and elders mock Christ by saying, "He saved others; himself he cannot save." Associating these words with the British soldiers signifies that they are the Christs of the modern world on whose shoulders the fate of the crown rests. But if the burden of salvation is transferred from God to man, it is not because of any permanence inherent in individual man. The last stanza is explicit in contrasting the stability of the crown with the mortality of man:

> Oh, God will save her, fear you not:
> Be you the men you've been,
> Get you the sons your fathers got,
> And God will save the Queen.
>
> (ll. 29–32)

The physical fact of generation, men passing into and out of existence, is thus seen as the basis for the preservation of the crown. Man, considered generically, attains a sort of permanence only in reproducing his own kind. Individual man must, therefore, get the sons his father got; and the act of generation, the acceptance of his own individual mortality, becomes man's only basis for any kind of permanence. Thus, "1887" introduces *A Shropshire Lad* into its proper setting of time and place and suggests the theme which is more fully explored in the poems that follow.

One need look no further than Lyric II, "Loveliest of Trees,"[5] to find the most explicit and direct statement of this theme. Whereas in "1887" it served as an underlying assumption in a poem about the celebration of Victoria's Golden Jubilee, in "Loveliest of Trees" it is the sole consideration of the poem. On the surface the poem is the most simple of poetic utterances. It opens with an image from nature which seems to suggest no more than the beauty of life at its prime:

> Loveliest of trees, the cherry now
> Is hung with bloom along the bough,
> And stands about the woodland ride
> Wearing white for Eastertide.
>
> (ll. 1–4)

---

[5] Because the majority of the poems of *A Shropshire Lad* are untitled, and because the position of the individual poem is often crucial to my argument, I have adopted the practice of referring to a poem as *Lyric II* or *No. II*, for example, rather than by the first line, i.e., "Loveliest of Trees," as is the more common procedure. However, I have varied this practice to avoid monotony when the context of my discussion makes clear the position of the poem in the over-all design of the work.

But the image has an ironic effect on the observer; it reminds him of his own mortality:

> Now, of my threescore years and ten,
> Twenty will not come again,
> And take from seventy springs a score,
> It only leaves me fifty more.
>
> (ll. 5–8)

His reaction is further complicated by the last stanza, for instead of producing a languid pessimism in the face of certain death, the realization of his transience results in an intensification of the speaker's perception:

> And since to look at things in bloom
> Fifty springs are little room,
> About the woodlands I will go
> To see the cherry hung with snow.
>
> (ll. 9–12)

The surface statement of the poem is thus simple: life is beautiful but it is short; and since it is short, one must enjoy it now. Translated into these terms, the poem seems commonplace, even insignificant. But Housman's treatment of the theme is not as bare as it first appears. The simplicity of the poem may be traced to the pastoral mode. The situation is perceived through the eyes of the Shropshire lad himself, a modern pastoral figure. The simplicity of the poem, through its subtle allusions to a more primitive version, reinforces the account of the loss of innocence it records. The cherry, "loveliest of trees," is, in a real sense, the tree of knowledge in the poem, and the subtle changes in the images associated with it chart a movement from innocence to knowledge. After its introduction in lines 1 and 2, the cherry tree is mentioned three times. In line 4 it is spoken of as "wearing white for Eastertide," in line 9 it is referred to as a thing "in bloom," and in the last line of the poem it is said to be "hung with snow." These three images, taken separately, could be considered merely conventional descriptions of white blooms; but taken in order, they suggest something more.

What they suggest has been debated. One critic has held that the snow image carries with it the suggestion of winter and death, merely continuing the association with death that "Eastertide" had introduced in the first stanza;[6] another has argued that *snow* is, in a poetic sense, no more than "a mass of white petals," and further that the association of Easter with death is "sheer perversion, for if Easter has any meaning, it is resurrection and immortal life."[7] While it is certainly true that Easter, as a poetic symbol, has been traditionally associated with springtime and rebirth, not winter and death, it is also true that a phrase such as "hung with snow," whatever its strict poetic definition, cannot be separated from the meanings which cling to it through traditional associations. The phrases "wearing white for Eastertide" and "hung with snow" are both clearly descriptive of the whiteness of the cherry blossom; but the images cannot be limited, in this case, to color associations, and snow carries with it further associations with winter and death as surely as Easter carries with it the notions of spring and rebirth.

What has been ignored is that the "snow" of the last line derives its full symbolic meaning from the structure of the poem. The image pattern progresses from spring ("wearing white for Eastertide") to summer ("things in bloom") to winter ("hung with snow"); or, if one prefers, from rebirth, to growth, to death.[8] It is clear that this is a progression, not in the scene observed—which remains constant—but in the perception of the young man who observes with Keatsian insight

[6] Winifred Lynskey, "Housman's 'Loveliest of Trees,' " *Explicator*, IV (1945–46), Item 59.

[7] W. L. Werner, "Housman's 'Loveliest of Trees,' " *Explicator*, V (1946–47), Item 4.

[8] The editors of the *Explicator* have noted, in connection with this reading of the poem, that Housman equates the spring with the first twenty years of life and winter with the last fifty years (I [1942–43], Item 57).

that the "loveliest" aspects of nature are the most melancholy, for they reveal a world in decay. It is also significant that the first lyric of *A Shropshire Lad* after the introductory poem depicts a symbolic tree of knowledge which leads the speaker from a view of a springtime world of rebirth to one "hung with snow." This revelation is, in essence, the central fact of *A Shropshire Lad*. Almost everything which follows has its basis in this thematic statement.

The third lyric, "The Recruit," completes the initial statement of the theme, and the poem's structure closely parallels that of "Loveliest of Trees." It too is marked by a duplicity of tone which cloaks its more complex attitude with a deceptively simple statement. The speaker wishes a young soldier well on his departure from Shropshire and assures him that he will not be forgotten "While Ludlow tower shall stand" (l. 4). The proverbial force of this line, which is repeated with slight variations throughout the poem, suggests on the surface the permanence of the recruit's fame in his home shire. The poem is complicated, however, by the subtle progression involved in the repetition of the refrain. In line 16 "While Ludlow tower shall stand" has become "Till Ludlow tower shall fall." The last line of the poem completes the progression, as the recruit is told, ". . . town and field will mind you / Till Ludlow tower is down." In meaning the three lines are the same; it is only in the movement of the refrain that Housman suggests the fall of the tower and introduces an element of irony into the poem. The irony lies in the contradiction between the truth of the speaker's remarks to the recruit—that he will be long remembered—and the qualification that the poem's structure implies—that his glory, like Ludlow tower, is impermanent in a world of constant change.

Housman's structuring principle in this poem, as in "Loveliest of Trees" and, to some extent, "1887," is the manipulation of the central image or refrain in such a manner that an early state of certainty gives way to a final attitude of uncertainty or disillusionment. Just as the certainty that "God will save the Queen" is qualified in "1887," and the vision of a world at its prime is replaced by the reality of death in "Loveliest of Trees," the belief in any kind of stability in life is undermined in "The Recruit." This structure, which moves from a naïve sense of permanence to an awareness of change, is one of the most pronounced architectonic patterns in *A Shropshire Lad.*

Lyric V, which uses this same pattern in its basic form, also has an element of the *carpe diem* theme of "Loveliest of Trees." The emphasis here is on the illusiveness of time, as pointed up by its being used as the chief argument of a young lover as he attempts a seduction. The dominant sense of time in the poem is further suggested by the flower imagery. In the first stanza the dandelions "tell the hours / That never are told again" (ll. 3–4) . In stanza 2 the youth links the flower image to his argument: "What flowers to-day may flower to-morrow, / But never as good as new" (ll. 13–14) . Finally, in stanza 4 he sighs, "Ah, life, what is it but a flower?" (l. 29) . The poem is set in springtime, with its promise of fulfillment:

> Ah, spring was sent for lass and lad,
> 'Tis now the blood runs gold,
> And man and maid had best be glad
> Before the world is old.
> (ll. 9–12)

Yet in Housman's world the promise of youth must yield to the discovery that all things, even human affection, are transient, as seen in the last two lines of each stanza of the poem, in which the entreaties of the youth become increasingly more urgent and the replies of the young girl increasingly more skeptical. Stanza 1 ends with "—'Twill do no harm to take my arm. / 'You may, young man, you may' "; stanza 2, "—Suppose I wound my arm right round— / ' 'Tis true, young man, 'tis true' "; stanza 3, "My love is true and all for you. / 'Perhaps, young man, perhaps' "; and stanza 4 culminates in, "Be kind, have pity, my own, my pretty.— / 'Good-bye, young man, good-bye' " Following the pattern established in the preceding lyrics, the poem begins with a naïve belief in the essential beauty and goodness of the world which is shattered at the end. This progression from innocence to something approaching insight, or the experience which leads to insight, is perhaps the most evident manifestation of the dominant theme of *A Shropshire Lad*.

The four poems just discussed further introduce three of the four distinct roles the persona assumes in the work—the naïve country lad, the soldier, and the lover. These, along with another persistent figure, the young criminal, make up the dramatis personae of *A Shropshire Lad*. Critics have long tried to account for Housman's obsession with certain types of characters, particularly the soldier and the criminal. Most of the explanations are, as one might expect, biographical. The most recent attempt to explain Housman's soldiers concludes that they represent no more than the current preoccupation of his countrymen: ". . . his imagination, which was stimulated by soldiery and warlike items, was mechanically controlled and held in line by his adherence to the public images of militarism."[9] However, critics have also explained away Housman's attraction to the soldier in the belief that a soldier is "often susceptible to his own sex," and the theory that Housman yearned toward "the gallant bearing and ripe masculinity of men in uniform."[10] Accordingly, Housman's young criminals and distraught lovers have been traced to some secret sense of guilt on the part of the poet.

John Stevenson's view that all of these figures are identical with "the only character of the poems, the Shropshire lad,"[11] may be true, but it does not answer the more basic question of why Housman chose to deal with these particular types. However, Stevenson does make an effort to explain why the rustic personality is central to the meaning of the poems:

[9] Robert Brainard Pearsall, "The Vendible Values of Housman's Soldiery," *PMLA*, LXXXII (1967), 85, 89.

[10] Watson, p. 145.

[11] Stevenson, p. 69.

If the theme of the response of innocence to experience and to action is the right one, it helps to place the Shropshire lad in a more dramatic position; his effect on the reader is more than a "literary" example of childish petulance and rebellion against society. We have only to turn to the poetry, to point out specific situations, to perceive that the "lad" of the poems, whether soldier, lover, or sinner, is himself a discoverer. Almost always Housman presents him at the moment when reality is made apparent, forever after which he must, like Mithridates, "sample all the killing store," and forever after which he knows that "happiness" and "pleasure" are illusions, that life, while perhaps not a sham, is something of a hoax, and that meaning comes only through struggle.[12]

But what, specifically, do the criminal, the lover, and the soldier discover? After examining poems in which these characters figure prominently, one must conclude that, although they have much in common, they represent three distinct aspects of the theme of discovery in *A Shropshire Lad*.

The poems dealing with young criminals and sinners serve, on the whole, to intensify the mythical sense of man's fallen state after the loss of innocence. He is now burdened, for the first time, with the realization of his own individual guilt and the general corruption of his world. Furthermore, the effect of these poems is to telescope into one moment of time the transformation from life at its prime to death. The death which the young murderer of Lyric IX faces, for example, is not distant and unreal, but imminent:

> They hang us now in Shrewsbury jail:
> The whistles blow forlorn,
> And trains all night groan on the rail
> To men that die at morn.
>
> (ll. 9–12)

The pathetic fallacy of these lines emphasizes the change that occurs in the outlook of one for whom death has become a real-

---

12 *Ibid.*, p. 80.

ity, a part of the conscious. Death, accordingly, is localized in time in the poem: ". . . he will hear the stroke of eight / And not the stroke of nine" (ll. 27–28) .

The more mythical element of the criminal poems is seen in Lyric VIII, which depicts in a dramatic monologue a murderer's departure from the land of his youth after his crime:

> "Farewell to barn and stack and tree,
>   Farewell to Severn shore.
> Terence, look your last at me,
>   For I come home no more.
>
> "The sun burns on the half-mown hill,
>   By now the blood is dried;
> And Maurice amongst the hay lies still
>   And my knife is in his side."
>
> (ll. 1-8)

The poem has been condemned for its "cheap theatrics" and "disagreeable melodramatics,"[13] but the basic elements of the narrative may be traced all the way back to the story of Cain and Abel, which the poem recalls.[14] Stanza 3 reveals that the murderer and his victim are brothers:

> "My mother thinks us long away;
>   'Tis time the field were mown.
> She had two sons at rising day,
>   To-night she'll be alone."
>
> (ll. 9–12)

With quick strokes the speaker fills in other details of the motif of Cain and Abel. In " 'Long for me the rick will wait, / And long will wait the fold' " and " 'We'll sweat no more on scythe and rake, / My bloody hands and I,' " the speaker says he is a farmer and, by contrasting the farmer's rick with the shepherd's fold, implies that Maurice, the murdered brother, was a

---

[13] See Frank Sullivan, "Housman's 'Farewell to Barn and Stack and Tree,' " *Explicator*, II (1943–44) , Item 36.

[14] This parallel was first noted by R. T. R., "Housman's 'Farewell to Barn and Stack and Tree,' " *Explicator*, I (1942–43) , Query 29.

shepherd. As the story of Cain and Abel recounts in the most vivid terms the consequences of the Fall, so this poem, by forcefully evoking the myth, intensifies that moment when man takes on the guilt he has inherited from his father. As Housman expresses it in Lyric XXVIII, in an entirely different context,

> When shall I be dead and rid
> Of the wrong my father did?
> How long, how long, till spade and hearse
> Put to sleep my mother's curse?
>
> (ll. 33–36)

One further element of the mythical account of the loss of innocence is the departure from the land which symbolized that innocence, exemplified by the expulsion of Adam and Eve from Eden and the wanderings of Cain. This motif becomes, in the pastoral tradition, the exile from the pastoral Arcadia and is exemplified in Lyric VIII by the murderer's departure from Shropshire. What later becomes the dominant structural motif for the whole work is found here in its archetypal form.

Lyric XLVII, "The Carpenter's Son," also reveals Housman employing traditional Biblical symbols in poems dealing with young criminals. The carpenter's son is clearly a pastoral version of Christ. He is to be hanged between two thieves, and he "hangs for love." Yet Housman's Christ figure in this poem, like the soldiers of "1887," represents a qualification of orthodox Christian thought. Just as the soldiers in Lyric I are used to emphasize the physical rather than the spiritual basis of life, "The Carpenter's Son" modifies the pattern traditionally associated with Christ's crucifixion. Instead of a Christ who dies magnanimously that others may be saved, who redeems man from the guilt incurred at the Fall, Housman's poem represents the carpenter's son as regretting his own loss of innocence, for experience has taught him that his efforts to change the nature of man were futile:

> "Oh, at home had I but stayed
> 'Prenticed to my father's trade,

23

Had I stuck to plane and adze,
I had not been lost, my lads.

"Then I might have built perhaps
Gallows-trees for other chaps,
Never dangled on my own,
Had I but left ill alone."

(ll. 5–12)

S. G. Andrews has pointed out that Housman's use of the
Biblical allusion in the poem represents a reversal of the traditional poetic use of allusion. Instead of adding to the meaning
of the situation described in the poem, Housman's allusion to
Christ points back to the original act of crucifixion and asks
the reader to reinterpret its significance in the light of the concept of man represented in *A Shropshire Lad*. Andrews states:

> It is significant that Housman's repeated allusions to
> Christ do not help us to understand the carpenter's son or
> his fate. Instead, they encourage us to transfer the speech
> of the carpenter's son to the mouth of Christ and to search
> for a sense in which the speech might apply to Him.[15]

It appears, then, that "The Carpenter's Son," like "1887," attempts to re-define a spiritual concept in strictly humanistic
terms. Housman's Christ is a disillusioned man who is faced
with the vanity of his efforts in the light of his knowledge of the
true nature of man. As Andrews notes, the lesson the poem
draws from the life of Christ is that it is futile to attempt to
change man's nature, to war with evil; the mature man has
learned to accept it as an inevitable condition in a transitory
and imperfect world. Housman's Christ has accepted at his
death the essential mortality of man, and the only promise he
is able to leave to his comrades is that they will face a better
death than he now faces:

"Make some day a decent end,
Shrewder fellows than your friend.

15 "Housman's 'The Carpenter's Son,' " *Explicator*, XIX (1960–61),
Item 3.

24

Fare you well, for ill fare I:
Live, lads, and I will die."

(ll. 25–28)

The condemned criminals of *A Shropshire Lad,* in common
with the other characters, make the tragic discovery of man's
impermanence in the face of immediate death, not a distant
one delayed by "fifty springs." Moreover, they symbolize the
burden of the human guilt which comes with knowledge. The
speaker of Lyric XXX declares:

Others, I am not the first,
Have willed more mischief than they durst:
If in the breathless night I too
Shiver now, 'tis nothing new.

(ll. 1–4)

They serve, finally, to compress into one dramatic moment in
time a process which is never so sharply defined in life. The
poetic advantages of these figures are obvious, both in establish-
ing the tone of the poems and in providing ready-made symbols
for lost innocence. Housman's criminals may thus be explained
more easily and more satisfactorily in terms of his art than in
terms of his life. If Housman expresses guilt, it is the mythic
guilt of the race, not merely his own.

The symbolic function of Housman's soldiers parallels, in
some respects, that of his criminals, except that while the criminal is a shameful figure, the soldier is always regarded with admiration, although it is sometimes an admiration tinged with
irony. In "1887," the soldiers are glorified as men who, in the
labor of preserving the state, "shared the work with God"; yet
they are "saviours" who could not even save themselves. The
young recruit of the third lyric, too, is a glorified figure who
will be remembered, the narrator tells him, "Till Ludlow tower
shall fall"; but his unspoken thought is that the recruit's fame
is destined to be short-lived. This dualism is partially explained
when one realizes that the soldier in the world of *A Shropshire
Lad* is mortal man stripped of all superfluous trappings, and his

tragic dilemma lies in recognizing that his ultimate duty is to
die. Lyric XXII demonstrates this symbolic function:

> The street sounds to the soldiers' tread,
>   And out we troop to see:
> A single redcoat turns his head,
>   He turns and looks at me.
>
> My man, from sky to sky's so far,
>   We never crossed before;
> Such leagues apart the world's ends are,
>   We're like to meet no more;
>
> What thoughts at heart have you and I
>   We cannot stop to tell;
> But dead or living, drunk or dry,
>   Soldier, I wish you well.

The narrator's obvious respect for the soldier in the poem is
not based on individual qualities; the soldier is a stranger, and
he cannot stop to disclose his own thoughts. The speaker's attitude is based instead on the generic qualities of the soldier.
Robert Brainard Pearsall has labeled these qualities "duty,
friendship, bravery."[16] but surely these are only the surface
clichés of a more fundamental quality. Poems such as "1887"
and "The Recruit" show that Housman refused to adopt the
jingoistic patriotism of many of his contemporaries. His attitude is always more complex than this easy answer would indicate. To look for the answer in Housman's personal attraction
to the masculinity represented by the soldiers is also irrelevant
to an understanding of the art of his poetry. The only answer
that satisfies the demands of criticism completely is the one
which locates the meaning of these figures within the framework of the poetry.

The preceding poem has shown that the soldier is respected
simply because he is a soldier, because he has accepted the consequences of being what he is. These consequences are ampli-
fied in the other war poems as seen in the first two stanzas of

[16] Pearsall, p. 90.

26

Lyric XXXV, which depict soldiers following the sound of drums to certain death:

> On the idle hill of summer,
>   Sleepy with the flow of streams,
> Far I hear the steady drummer
>   Drumming like a noise in dreams.
>
> Far and near and low and louder
>   On the roads of earth go by,
> Dear to friends and food for powder,
>   Soldiers marching, all to die.
>
>   (ll. 1-8)

This view of man, seen as the soldier, is the dominant one of *A Shropshire Lad*. The fate of the soldier and the fate of man is to march to an inevitable death. The figure of the soldier embodies Housman's paradoxical attitude toward this process; for the soldier, symbolizing the man who willingly accepts this fate, is both a heroic figure and a pitiful one. Line 7, "Dear to friends and food for powder," recalls Falstaff's description of the men he leads into battle. "Tut, tut, good enough to toss, food for powder, food for powder; they'll fill a pit as well as better; tush, man, mortal men, mortal men" (*Henry IV, Part I*, IV, ii, 56–58). The poet's own attitude seems to be a mixture of the realistic view of Falstaff and the more heroic stance of Hotspur. Housman has not arrived at the realism of Wilfred Owen or Stephen Spender, but he can lament the pity of it all. Stanza 3 of the poem is a stark, if somewhat romanticized, picture of the forgotten dead:

> East and west on fields forgotten
>   Bleach the bones of comrades slain,
> Lovely lads and dead and rotten;
>   None that go return again.
>
>   (ll. 9–12)

The elemental dichotomy between life and death and the inevitability of man's approach to death ("None that go return again") establish the almost allegorical tone of the war poems.

The last stanza of Lyric XXXV suggests something of the motivation behind the soldier's symbolic march into battle. Here the speaker is drawn by the sounds of the march:

> Far the calling bugles hollo,
> > High the screaming fife replies,
> Gay the files of scarlet follow:
> Woman bore me, I will rise.
>
> (ll. 13–16)

The apparent causal relationship between "woman bore me" and "I will rise" defines the nature of the march and of the man who makes it. The soldier rises to answer the call of war only because "woman bore me"; the act of creation implies the acceptance of ultimate destruction. The poet's preoccupation with the soldier, evident throughout *A Shropshire Lad,* may thus be traced in part to the fact that the soldier represents man in his most elemental form, journeying toward his confrontation with death.

Two concluding war poems, Lyrics LVI and LX, reinforce this interpretation of Housman's soldiers. Lyric LVI deals with the futility of man's attempt to escape his fate. It is entitled "The Day of Battle," and it depicts the dilemma which confronts the soldier:

> "Far I hear the bugle blow
> To call me where I would not go,
> And the guns begin the song,
> 'Soldier, fly or stay for long.' "
>
> (ll. 1–4)

The choice between cowardice and death that is presented in the first stanza dictates the structure of the remaining three stanzas; each is stated as one step of a logical argument (if . . . but since . . . therefore):

> "Comrade, if to turn and fly
> Made a soldier never die,
> Fly I would, for who would not?
> 'Tis sure no pleasure to be shot.

"But since the man that runs away
Lives to die another day,
And cowards' funerals, when they come,
Are not wept so well at home,

"Therefore, though the best is bad,
Stand and do the best, my lad;
Stand and fight and see your slain,
And take the bullet in your brain."

(ll. 5–16)

The crux of the argument lies in lines 9 and 10. The inevitability of death makes desertion merely a cowardly delaying tactic. The soldier is thus left with the decision to " 'stand and do the best,' " to accept the fate of being a soldier, which involves facing death squarely without flinching.

Lyric LX, too, concentrates on the death which is the inevitable fate of Housman's soldier, though more subtly:

Now hollow fires burn out to black,
And lights are guttering low:
Square your shoulders, lift your pack,
And leave your friends and go.

Oh never fear, man, nought's to dread,
Look not left nor right:
In all the endless road you tread
There's nothing but the night.

Housman's structure, contrasting light and dark, has the effect of driving home the meaning although leaving the central theme of death unexpressed.[17] He accomplishes this effect in Lyric LX by a fusion of pattern and meaning. The final line ("There's nothing but the night") becomes completely clear only when the reader accepts the implications of the light-dark imagery. Likewise, the poem's argument (since death is inevitable, it is not to be feared) is nowhere stated but nevertheless present.

The one common feature of all the war poems is this con-

17 See Schneider, pp. 95–96.

cern with the inevitability of man's fate and the courage with which it is confronted by the scarlet-clad soldiers of the Queen. It is a courage not frequently shared by the young lovers, the third major group of characters who inhabit the world of Shropshire. Michael Macklem has noted Housman's frequent use of love as a traditional symbol of the intensity and brevity of happiness.[18] Stevenson has spoken of Housman's lover as one who, "aware of the inevitability of death and decay, aware of the ambiguity of honor and love, accepts the moment of fulfillment as the only reality."[19] Yet, as Stevenson further states, the lover in Housman's poetry soon discovers the transitory nature of love, and his commitment ends in frustration. It is thus that love frequently functions as a basis for the treatment of human transience in Housman's poetry. The ideal love of one-and-twenty, characterized by a sense of permanence, is replaced by the disillusionment of two-and-twenty:

> When I was one-and-twenty
> I heard a wise man say,
> "Give crowns and pounds and guineas
> But not your heart away;
> Give pearls away and rubies
> But keep your fancy free."
> But I was one-and-twenty,
> No use to talk to me.
>
> When I was one-and-twenty
> I heard him say again,
> "The heart out of the bosom
> Was never given in vain;
> 'Tis paid with sighs a plenty
> And sold for endless rue."
> And I am two-and-twenty,
> And oh, 'tis true, 'tis true.
>
> (Lyric XIII)

18 Macklem, p. 44.
19 Stevenson, p. 81.

The discovery which is significant in the poem is that love is of a different nature from "crowns and pounds and guineas"; the difference is underlined by the imagery of buying and selling. The "wise man" knows that pearls and rubies may be given away but not the heart; it is, in fact, impossible to give away, for something is always gotten in return. The heart is always *sold*, and the price is "endless rue." The poem conveys the suddenness of this discovery by delaying the revelation until the last line: "And oh, 'tis true, 'tis true."

Housman further implements the close correlation between love and the theme of the impermanence of human existence by his constant identification of love and death. Tom Burns Haber, noting this interweaving of the two experiences, states: "When Housman mentions the sex-embrace he usually casts the odor of death around it."[20] Three consecutive poems, Lyrics XXV, XXVI, and XXVII, illustrate the poet's fusion of love and death. All three poems deal with a triangle of lovers in which one is now in the grave. Lyric XXVII depicts the inconstancy of love with the unrealistic situation of a dead lover speaking from the grave. The poem alternates the dead man's questions and his friend's answers:

> "Is my team ploughing,
>   That I was used to drive
> And hear the harness jingle
>   When I was man alive?"
>
> Ay, the horses trample,
>   The harness jingles now;
> No change though you lie under
>   The land you used to plough.
>   (ll. 1–8)

The first four stanzas serve to emphasize the changelessness of the scene the dead man has left. The cycle of life has continued unaltered: "No change though you lie under / The land you

20 "A. E. Housman's Downward Eye," *JEGP*, LIII (1954), 312.

used to plough." This contrast between the permanence of generic man and the mutability of individual man, a concern of many of Housman's love poems, is continued in the last four stanzas with added force as the dead man shifts his attention to his sweetheart and his friend. He inquires about the happiness of the surviving lover and asks if she has " 'tired of weeping / As she lies down at eve' " (ll. 19–20), only to be told:

> Aye, she lies down lightly,
>   She lies not down to weep:
> Your girl is well contented.
>   Be still, my lad, and sleep.
>   (ll. 21–24)

But the dead man will not be still, and his innocent queries lead inevitably to the revelation of the final stanzas:

> "Is my friend hearty,
>   Now I am thin and pine,
> And has he found to sleep in
>   A better bed than mine?"
>
> Yes, lad, I lie easy,
>   I lie as lads would choose;
> I cheer a dead man's sweetheart,
>   Never ask me whose.
>   (ll. 25–32)

The last stanza emphasizes the paradox that is inherent in the poem, for in asserting the permanence of the life that the dead man has left, his friend has also acknowledged the transience of individual man. The friend and the sweetheart remain unchanged, but only at the expense of the dead lover. The poem thus reveals Housman's use of love as a symbol of change. It deals with two kinds of love—the love of a friend and the love of a sweetheart. The dead youth's questions (ll. 13–16) reveal his naïveté, seeing love as fixed and unchanging. He asks if his sweetheart has "tired of weeping," as if physical exhaustion were the only force which could end her grief. His naïveté is also revealed in the ambiguity of his desire that his friend has found "a better bed" to sleep in. The poem's last stanza, however, destroys the dead youth's notion of love's permanence as an illusion. Love, like life, is marked by an inconstancy and a brevity which is emphasized further by the juxtaposition of the lover and the grave which characterizes this poem and the two which precede it.

Lyric XXV depicts the same situation from a different point of view—that of the lover who steals a dead man's sweetheart ("When Rose and I walk out together / Stock-still lies Fred and sleeps"), and Lyric XXVI completes the triangle by projecting the affair from the third point of view—that of the lover who accepts a new sweetheart after the death of the old one:

> Along the field as we came by
> A year ago, my love and I,
> The aspen over stile and stone
> Was talking to itself alone.
> "Oh who are these that kiss and pass?
> A country lover and his lass;
> Two lovers looking to be wed;
> And time shall put them both to bed,
> But she shall lie with earth above,
> And he beside another love."
>
> (ll. 1–10)

The last stanza of the poem reveals that the forecast of the aspen tree, a traditional symbol of prophecy, has indeed been fulfilled: "And sure enough beneath the tree / There walks another love with me" (ll. 11–12). However, the poem further strengthens its characterization of love's inconstancy by suggesting an endless cycle of lovers forgotten in death and betrayed by the surviving lovers:

> And overhead the aspen heaves
> Its rainy-sounding silver leaves;
> And I spell nothing in their stir,
> But now perhaps they speak to her,

33

And plain for her to understand
They talk about a time at hand
When I shall sleep with clover clad,
And she beside another lad.

(ll. 13-20)

These three poems, affording shifting perspectives of the same theme, illustrate on a small scale the sense of continuity which characterizes the whole of *A Shropshire Lad*. Each is concerned with the destructive power of time, and each develops its theme by concentrating on the ephemeral nature of those feelings and emotions which are traditionally regarded as the most enduring—love and the memory of the dead. But the sense of the cruelty of time is strengthened in each of the poems by Housman's depiction of the transience of the individual against the background of the permanence of his class. All three poems are built on this contrast; the pattern of life continues for the living, and the dead are soon forgotten.

The unity observed in these lyrics may be noted in all of the poems of *A Shropshire Lad* dealing with young lovers. Each depicts something of the cruelty of time, the disillusionment of the man who places his trust in the stability of human experiences and emotions. "Bredon Hill," Lyric XXI, is structured on the pattern which molds many of the lyrics of the work. It opens "In summertime on Bredon," with a scene suggestive of the joy of young love; but in the course of the poem the early hope of youth is extinguished by death, and there is a corresponding transition from summer to winter, "when the snows at Christmas / On Bredon top were strown." The poem contains yet another pattern of imagery through which the theme of lost innocence is developed—the church bells which sound through the shires:

In summertime on Bredon
  The bells they sound so clear;
Round both the shires they ring them

> In steeples far and near,
> A happy noise to hear.
>
> (ll. 1–5)

The two young lovers who lie on Bredon Hill on Sunday morning resist the call of the bells as a summons to worship, reinterpreting it as a symbol of the fulfillment of their love:

> The bells would ring to call her
> In valleys miles away:
> "Come all to church, good people;
> Good people, come and pray."
> But here my love would stay.
>
> And I would turn and answer
> Among the springing thyme,
> "Oh, peal upon our wedding,
> And we will hear the chime,
> And come to church in time."
>
> (ll. 11–20)

But in stanza 6 the bells, like the cherry tree of Lyric II, are presented in a new light; they have become funeral bells, for the young man's love "stole out unbeknown / And went to church alone." The sound, which in youth and innocence was "a happy noise to hear" and a symbol of promise, has become, through the experience of death by which the lad has discovered the vanities of love and of life, a call to death—a call which the youth now realizes he too must answer:

> The bells they sound on Bredon,
> And still the steeples hum.
> "Come all to church, good people,"—
> Oh, noisy bells, be dumb;
> I hear you, I will come.
>
> (ll. 31–35)

"The True Lover" (Lyric LIII) again centers on the inconstancy of love with what appear to be symbolic implications. The poem, concerned with the suicide of a young lover, has intrigued commentators with its cryptic style. Brooks, Purser, and Warren talk of the poem's "symbolic force" and its ability to project "something beyond itself."[21] Maude M. Hawkins also finds that the suicide "may be entirely symbolic."[22] Much of the poem's force lies in its effective use of the ballad form. It is stripped of all but the most significant details, with no attempt at characterization; and the true nature of the situation described is not immediately given but is revealed by degrees so that it is not until the last line of the poem that one is able to interpret (or perhaps reinterpret) the ambiguous title and to understand the phrase that is repeated in the poem: "When lovers crown their vows."

With a simplicity that is more apparent than real, the poem deals with a lover who desires to see his sweetheart (who has presumably rejected him) once more before he departs for some unnamed destination:

> The lad came to the door at night,
>   When lovers crown their vows,
> And whistled soft and out of sight
>   In shadow of the boughs.
>
> "I shall not vex you with my face
>   Henceforth, my love, for aye;
> So take me in your arms a space
>   Before the east is grey.
>
> "When I from hence away am past
>   I shall not find a bride,
> And you shall be the first and last
>   I ever lay beside."
>
>   (ll. 1–12)

It is not until stanza 5 that the reader discovers the true nature of the lad's journey. The first suggestions come through the sweetheart's questions:

> "Oh do you breathe, lad, that your breast

21 Cleanth Brooks, John Thibaut Purser, and Robert Penn Warren, *An Approach to Literature* (New York, 1952), pp. 296–97.
22 "Houseman's 'The True Lover,'" *Explicator*, VIII (1949–50).

> Seems not to rise and fall,
> And here upon my bosom prest
> There beats no heart at all?
>
> . . . .
>
> "Oh lad, what is it, lad, that drips
> Wet from your neck on mine?
> What is it falling on my lips,
> My lad, that tastes of brine?"
>
> (ll. 17–20, 25–28)

The lad's answers, which reveal that his heart has stopped and " 'never goes again' " and that his throat has been cut, only make more emphatic the point which has already become clear—that his is a journey of death. Realizing this fact, one may well wonder at Housman's purpose in depicting such an unrealistic situation. Yet the death of the young lover is crucial to the theme of the poem. Darrell Abel's analysis finds that the poem's real center is the assumption that human nature is incapable of an enduring passion. The true lover of the poem's title is one whose love never ceases, but a knowledge of the inconstancy of love brings with it the realization that the lover must eventually break his vow. Therefore, the lover in this poem "remains true by adopting the desperately logical expedient of suicide at the consummating moment of love."[23] With this interpretation in mind, we may note, again following Abel's analysis, that the line which is repeated in the poem, "When lovers crown their vows," takes on new meaning. In the opening stanza the line may be read conventionally as suggesting the lovers' promise to consummate the act of love. But through the course of the poem, Housman has again[24] redefined the line so that when it appears as the last line of the poem, it refers to the act of suicide as the true crowning of the vows of love. Thus the poem emphasizes the transitory nature of hu-

---

[23] *Ibid.,* Item 23.
[24] See, for example, Lyrics I and III, where Housman accomplishes the same effect of redefining a phrase through the course of the poem.

man emotions by suggesting that only by death is man freed from the inconstancy that characterizes life.[25] The "true lover" of the poem's title is now defined as a dead lover.

Not all of Housman's love lyrics are as serious in tone as the preceding analyses might indicate. Yet all of them are characterized by the same emphasis on inconstancy. The lover of Lyric XVIII is almost flippant in his attitude towards the inconstancy of love, yet even though the poem is light in tone and avoids Housman's customary association of love with death or suicide, it underscores his theme that "nothing will remain":

> Oh, when I was in love with you,
>   Then I was clean and brave,
> And miles around the wonder grew
>   How well did I behave.
>
> And now the fancy passes by,
>   And nothing will remain,
> And miles around they'll say that I
>   Am quite myself again.

Lyric VI contains something of the same lighthearted view of love. It treats love as an illness in the courtly love tradition, with the lover "Mute and dull of cheer and pale," lying "at death's own door." The maiden can "heal his ail," but at the risk of becoming infected herself. So transitory is the nature of love that if the lover's desires are fulfilled, his love is over, and it is the maiden who must "lie down forlorn":

> Buy them, buy them: eve and morn
>   Lovers' ills are all to sell.
> Then you can lie down forlorn;
>   But the lover will be well.
>   (ll. 9–16)

The imagery of buying and selling recurs here with the same implication as in Lyric XIII—love can never be given freely

---

[25] This point—that death provides a permanence which man is denied in life—is an important corollary to the mutability theme, and is discussed more completely in Ch. III.

but is always sold. The maiden must get something in return, in this case, the "wan look, the hollow tone, / The hung head, the sunken eye" (ll. 6–7). It is now she who is ill, for in transferring the ills of love, her lover has recovered. The process has thus come full circle, and the poem suggests the endless cycle for which the plague of love is responsible.

The cyclical pattern of the poem recalls that of Lyrics XXV, XXVI, and XXVII, which depict the shifting pattern of affection among a triangle of lovers, and that of "Bredon Hill," which makes use of the metaphor of the changing seasons to portray love's changefulness. The recurrence of this cyclical pattern in the love lyrics, as well as its frequent occurrence in the opening lyrics such as II, III, V, and VII, emphasizes Housman's use of a submerged metaphor for change to support his structural pattern.

Tom Burns Haber has noted the frequency of this cyclical structure in Housman's poetry.[26] For example, he quotes from Lyric XXXVI, which employs the metaphor of the circle, and states that in the two stanzas quoted below, Housman wrote "his poem of his poems"; or, as we are to understand, his poem that describes his poetic method:

> The world is round, so travellers tell,
> And straight though reach the track,
> Trudge on, trudge on, 'twill all be well,
> The way will guide one back.
>
> But ere the circle homeward hies
> Far, far must it remove:
> White in the moon the long road lies
> That leads me from my love.
>
> (ll. 9–16)

In discussing the structure of Housman's poetry Haber points out that, not only does Housman use the circle metaphorically, but he also creates a circular pattern by making one or more

[26] "A. E. Housman: Astronomer-Poet," *English Studies*, XXXV (1954), 154–58.

of the last lines of a poem identical with one or more of the first or, at times, by repeating a key word or phrase in the last line that was found in the opening lines of the poem. Yet Haber ignores the relationship between this structuring principle and the theme of Housman's poetry. He theorizes instead that Housman's interest in astronomy is responsible for his tendency to employ the circle as a frequent metaphor in his poems.[27] Housman's use of this form he regards as "the habituated movement of his mind, which did not act in tangential and parabolic patterns, symbols of the true maker."[28] Haber, in fact, is convinced that Housman's use of the pattern is detrimental to his poetry:

> As to form, these influences have not been fortunate: the stuff of poetry was too often subdued to what the scholar worked in. . . . When the poet's mind began to give form to the emotional flux, it too often was set spinning in the well-worn cycle. *Scit vox missa reverti.* Without his circles and ellipses the astronomer is nothing but they are death to poetry.[29]

However, Housman's poems are indeed parabolical in another nongeometric sense; the pattern of one lyric frequently acts as a parable, or symbol, of the theme that is predominant in the poems of *A Shropshire Lad.* For example, the circle, the central metaphor of Lyric XXXVI, with which Haber illustrates the cyclical pattern in Housman's poetry, depicts and reinforces the theme of life's pattern of endless change. Haber did not cite stanza 2 of the poem, which fuses the circle metaphor and the poem's theme:

> Still hangs the hedge without a gust,
> Still, still the shadows stay:

[27] Haber records that, as a child, Housman enjoyed playing a game which involved placing his two younger brothers on the lawn to illustrate the mechanics of the solar system. He maintained a lifelong interest in astronomy. The majority of his scholarly work was devoted to editing the five books of the *Astronomica* of Manilius.

[28] Haber, "A. E. Housman: Astronomer-Poet," p. 158.

[29] *Ibid.*

My feet upon the moonlit dust
Pursue the ceaseless way.

(ll. 5–8)

The image pattern of this stanza is a familiar one that occurs repeatedly in *A Shropshire Lad*. It contrasts ceaseless change with stability and permanence. In the first two lines the word *still* is used three times, and the phrase *without a gust* and the word *stay* also signify a motionlessness that is in sharp contrast to the lover's "ceaseless" pursuit of his cyclical journey. Housman indeed uses a circular structure for the whole poem. The last two lines of the poem are exactly the same as the first two lines, thus closing the circle of the poem's structure. But this structure seems to represent not merely an obsessive trait in the mind of the poet but a functional element of the poem, for the whole poem functions as an expressive metaphor of human transience, showing the lover's endless change against a backdrop of changelessness.

Perhaps a better illustration of the function of the cyclical structure—because the poem is more successful—is Lyric XXXI.

> On Wenlock Edge the wood's in trouble;
>   His forest fleece the Wrekin heaves;
> The gale, it plies the saplings double,
>   And thick on Severn snow the leaves.
>
> 'Twould blow like this through holt and hanger
>   When Uricon the city stood:
> 'Tis the old wind in the old anger,
>   But then it threshed another wood.
>
> Then, 'twas before my time, the Roman
>   At yonder heaving hill would stare:
> The blood that warms an English yeoman,
>   The thoughts that hurt him, they were there.
>
> There, like the wind through woods in riot,
>   Through him the gale of life blew high;
> The tree of man was never quiet:
>   Then 'twas the Roman, now 'tis I.

The gale, it plies the saplings double,
It blows so hard, 'twill soon be gone:
To-day the Roman and his trouble
Are ashes under Uricon.

A knowledge of the geographical references in the poem is helpful; Robert Stallman explains them as follows:

The Wrekin, near Shrewsbury and Wenlock in Salop or Shropshire, the region about Ludlow celebrated by Housman, is a solitary West-country hill over 1300 feet high. "It is interesting to the geologist," Murray's *Handbook of England and Wales* reports, "as being a remarkable example of eruptive trap. . . . There are traces of British camps on the summit, but they are much overgrown with plantations." Since the Wrekin was an extinct volcano "when Uricon the city stood," the ashes of the Roman under Uricon are not volcanic; they are the ashes simply of Roman and English yeomen levelled by Time and Fate.[30]

As Stallman implies, this poem is concerned with time but, more specifically, with the paradoxical notions of continuity and change in time. It has a much broader scope than the love lyrics, such as Lyric XVIII; its scene takes in centuries. The Wrekin is itself a symbol of both the change and continuity of time. Its slopes show evidence of the Roman city of Uricon, which has now been leveled by the decay of centuries. Yet the wind that blows now "through holt and hanger"[31] is the "old wind in the old anger" that blew through another wood when a Roman watched the saplings of the woods double. Thus both mutability and permanence are represented by the scene.

The poem also emphasizes the continuity of feeling which exists in generic man: "The blood that warms an English yeoman, / The thoughts that hurt him, they were there" [in the

[30] "Housman's 'On Wenlock Edge,' " *Explicator*, III (1944–45) , Item 26.
[31] The sense of antiquity is strengthened in the poem by Housman's use of the archaic words *holt* and *hanger,* both from the Anglo-Saxon word stock. *Hanger,* according to the *OED*, refers to "a wood on the side of a steep hill or bank." A holt is a wooded hill.

time of the Roman]. Yet within this continuity the poem reveals endless change. In line 16 the Englishman who watches
the wind riot through the woods acknowledges the cycle of
change which constitutes human existence: "Then 'twas the
Roman, now 'tis I." The last two lines of the poem are elo-
quent in their implication that the Englishman realizes the
significance of his discovery: "To-day the Roman and his trouble / Are ashes under Uricon." As Spiro Peterson has observed,[32]
line 16 almost echoes after the conclusion of the poem. That is,
the reader may be tempted to supply line 16 as the final line
of the poem. The Roman had his day and is now ashes under
Uricon; now 'tis I. The parallel between past and present is
complete, and the pattern of human existence has again come
full circle.

But the poem's structure is more complex than the preceding
analysis indicates. Peterson has pointed out two dominant motifs which run throughout the poem—the historical perspective
of man as symbolized by the hill and its ruins, and the close correlation between man and nature as depicted in the wind imagery, with the man-nature parallel reinforcing the past-
present parallel. The poem opens with a scene of a "woods in
riot." The forest "heaves"; the "saplings double"; the leaves
snow "thick on Severn." This disturbance parallels the emotional unrest of the observer (the Englishman, but, by implication, the Roman also), who watches the scene. The poem's
structure establishes this parallel by the fusion of the images
of man and the images of the wind-torn woods. Fused images
such as "gale of life" and "tree of man" link the two motifs. In
addition, Housman gives the wind human qualities in his ref-

[32] The "sense of the complete parallel, the logic of the poem, the structure of the stanza demand that the poem conclude with the same three
words [*now 'tis I*]. Like the Roman, the speaker (and 'his trouble') are soon
to be under the ashes of Wenlock. The Force, which meant disturbance or
change for nature, destruction for past civilization, now signifies oblivion
for the speaker himself. All the more conspicuous for their absence are the
expected words, 'now 'tis I.' " ("Housman's 'On Wenlock Edge,' " *Explicator*,
XV [1956-57], Item 46.)

erence to its "old anger." Thus the poem makes the further implication that the pattern of nature and the pattern of man's existence are imaged by the same cycle. Peterson finds that the poem's images

> reinforce the structure because they interpret the subject, namely, that physical and human nature are passive victims of a Force violent, but not malevolent . . . the poem says nature avoids complete destruction by an endless cyclical process—as does man. The Roman and his man-made Uricon are succeeded by the English yeoman and his Wenlock. Man succumbs to his never-quiet spirit, just as nature (wood, hill, river) meets its trouble, gale, old wind in the old anger.[33]

Lyric XXXI thus becomes another of the many expressions of the mutability theme in *A Shropshire Lad*. It also serves as an impressive argument against Haber's contention that Housman's cyclical structure is not a meaningful and necessary element in his poetic construction.[34] Lyric XXXI, like many of the other lyrics of *A Shropshire Lad*, demonstrates that Housman's structural motifs are inseparable from the poems' total meanings. The cyclical structure which recurs in the poems is an embodiment of Housman's treatment of the problem of change; it cannot be explained away merely by reference to his study of astronomy or a perversity of spirit.

Housman's commentators, with few exceptions, have tended to ignore the essential unity of theme which characterizes *A Shropshire Lad* and the close relationship which exists between this theme and the structural patterns of the poems. Yet it should be clear that a recognition of this unity is necessary for an understanding of his reliance on certain symbolic characters and incidents, as well as his reliance on certain recur-

33 *Ibid.*

34 In another essay, Haber labels Housman's structuring principles "perverse" in their tendency to destroy a scene of idyllic love or hope with a "cynical thrust" ("The Spirit of the Perverse in A. E. Housman," *South Atlantic Quarterly*, XL [1941], 368–78) .

ring architectonic principles. The theme is by no means restricted to the poems discussed in this chapter. Housman was not content merely to depict the state of lost innocence; *A Shropshire Lad* is also concerned with a quest for the recovery of innocence, as manifested in a search for permanence, a search so paradoxical in nature that it must be considered in some detail.

III

VARIATION: THE QUEST FOR PERMANENCE

*T*he concern with human transience is, of course, one of the great commonplaces of English poetry, and in many respects Housman's treatment of this theme is quite conventional. Like Shakespeare, he laments that "Golden lads and girls all must, / As chimney-sweepers, come to dust." He discovers, like Keats, death in the midst of beauty; and like Marvell and his contemporaries, he concludes in poems such as "Loveliest of Trees" that an awareness of the brevity of life leads to a desire to experience it more intensely. Yet a seemingly contradictory reaction to the consciousness of change may be observed in *A Shropshire Lad*. In many of the poems the recognition of transience and decay leads to the acceptance of death rather than a more vigorous participation in life. Lyric VII, for example, characterizes life as a cyclical process of change ended only by death. It asks: " 'What use to rise and rise? / Rise man a thousand mornings / Yet down at last he lies, . . .' " (ll. 12–14). And lines from the last stanza reinforce the inevitability of the process with this analogy: " 'The sun moves always west; / The road one treads to labour / Will lead one home to rest, . . .' " (ll. 27–29). And the persona adds in an acceptance of death as the end of the cycle: " 'And that will be the best.' "

In *A Shropshire Lad* two apparently conflicting reactions to the knowledge that comes with the loss of innocence emerge —on the one hand, an intensification of experience; on the other, a desire for the release of death. It is the second element of the theme that has led many critics to dismiss Housman as a bitter pessimist who, in his perversity, desires only to expose the evil and injustice of an existence that is not worth maintaining. However, a careful analysis of the poems in which these two aspects of the theme appear casts some doubt on this conclusion. It is clear, in fact, in examining the view of life represented by "Loveliest of Trees" that to regard Housman merely as a pessimist is to oversimplify a more complex attitude.

Lyric IV, entitled "Reveille," continues the motif established in "Loveliest of Trees." The poem's title suggests both its subject and its central metaphor. It is a call for action in the face of approaching death, and it develops its theme structurally through the controlling metaphor of the sun's passage from dawn to dusk:

> Wake: the silver dusk returning
>   Up the beach of darkness brims,
> And the ship of sunrise burning
>   Strands upon the eastern rims.
>
>   (ll. 1–4)

Housman's use of the conventional symbolic association of light with life and darkness with death has been noted earlier. Here the poem is constructed on the analogy of the journey of life and the journey of the sun from dawn to darkness, an apt, if not particularly original, comparison. But Housman keeps the poem from becoming commonplace by leaving the comparison unstated, although it does serve as the basis for the argument for action and involvement in youth before death removes the opportunity for action.

> Up, lad: thews that lie and cumber
>   Sunlit pallets never thrive;
> Morns abed and daylight slumber
>   Were not meant for man alive.
>
> Clay lies still, but blood's a rover;
>   Breath's a ware that will not keep.

47

Up, lad: when the journey's over
There'll be time enough to sleep.

(ll. 17–24)

The poem opens with dawn and closes with the suggestion of
falling night, paralleling "Loveliest of Trees" with its progression from springtime to winter; but in neither poem does the
consciousness that "breath's a ware that will not keep" lead to
a rejection of life, rather to an emphasis on the value of life at
its prime and to the necessity of an intense and vital existence.

To ignore this line of development is to risk misinterpreting
the view of life contained in *A Shropshire Lad,* and evidence
of such an oversimplification of Housman's poetry is not difficult to find. Hugh Molson, for example, states that Housman
regarded human life "as an unmerited ordeal which serves no
useful purpose but from which man obtains his final release
after death."[1] Stephen Spender finds that "the hanging, suicides, shooting, war, hemlock" of Housman's poems express his
feelings about "the wretchedness of life. . . ."[2] Edmund Wilson
writes that in Housman's poetry "we find only the realization
of man's smallness . . . of his own basic wrongness to himself,
his own inescapable anguish."[3] Yet clearly "Reveille" predi-
cates some value to life. It encourages a participation in life
even as it retains a consciousness of approaching death. Simi-
larly, at the end of "Loveliest of Trees" the speaker determines
to involve himself in the beauty of the world even though it
will forever more be "hung with snow," colored by the knowledge of death.

This view is not restricted to one or two poems. Lyric XXIV
calls for the same kind of involvement, and for exactly the same
reasons:

[1] "The Philosophies of Hardy and Housman," *Quarterly Review,*
CCLXVIII (1937), 205.
[2] "The Essential Housman" in *The Making of a Poem* (London, 1955),
p. 159.
[3] "A. E. Housman" in *The Triple Thinkers* (New York, 1948), p. 62.

> Say, lad, have you things to do?
>   Quick then, while your day's at prime.
> Quick, and if 'tis work for two,
>   Here am I, man: now's your time.
>
> (ll. 1–4)

Again the basis for action is the consciousness that ripeness implies decay:

> Use me ere they lay me low
>   Where a man's no use at all;
>
> Ere the wholesome flesh decay,
>   And the willing nerve be numb,
> And the lips lack breath to say,
>   "No, my lad, I cannot come."
>
> (ll. 7–12)

In Lyric XXXII, Housman again makes use of natural elements to suggest man's delicate grasp of his existence. He is like the wind that gathers from its twelve quarters, tarries "for a breath," then takes its "endless way." The realization that life is only a moment in an eternity of time serves to quicken the intensity of that moment: "Take my hand quick .... Speak now, and I will answer" (ll. 7, 9). The repetition of *quick*, cited in lines 2 and 3 of Lyric XXIV quoted above, achieves the same end, with a pun on the older meaning of the word. Finally, Lyric LVII is yet another expression of the value of life, even in the face of eternal death: "I shall have lived a little while / Before I die for ever" (ll. 7–8).

These poems clearly cast some doubt on the view that Housman regarded life as an "unmerited ordeal" from which death releases man, a view which implies that death is superior to life. The tone of Lyrics II, IV, XXIV, XXXII, and LVII weakens such a view; and in fact, it is possible to cite passages in *A Shropshire Lad* in which Housman states that life at its prime is far superior to death. In Lyric XXV the speaker states: "A lad that lives and has his will / Is worth a dozen dead" (ll. 11–12). Lyric XXXIII, for a further example, introduces the idea of prolonging life through love:

> If truth in hearts that perish
>   Could move the powers on high,
> I think the love I bear you
>   Should make you not to die.
>
> (ll. 1–4)

A number of the poems of *A Shropshire Lad* thus predicate a value to life not in spite of but almost because of its brevity. Yet this aspect of the work is in direct contradiction to the widely held view that Housman voices "a philosophy compounded of pessimism and defeat."[4] What is left then, seemingly, is the view that *A Shropshire Lad* is self-contradictory in its treatment of the relative values of life and death. A number of critics have felt that such is indeed the case. Jacob Bronowski states:

> Housman's poems reel from one standard to another. If one poem finds love worthy . . . the poem over the page will find it pointless. . . . If one poem is glad that a young man has left life before honour, the next will say that silly lads always want to leave their life.[5]

Hugh Molson also finds that Housman answers the question of the value of life and death in contradictory ways:

> The feeling that it is better to be alive than dead is vigorously expressed by a suitor who, rejected while his rival was alive, has survived him with satisfactory results. . . . Exactly the opposite opinion is expressed in another poem.[6]

J. B. Priestley writes:

> . . . his running grievance, on examination, can be resolved

---

[4] Louis Untermeyer, "A. E. Housman" in *Modern American Poetry; Modern British Poetry*, II, 101.

[5] "Alfred Edward Housman" in *The Poet's Defence* (Cambridge, 1939), pp. 222–23.

[6] Molson, pp. 207–208.

into two separate complaints that are not at all consistent; in the first, life is lovely enough, but all too short, and death is the enemy of happiness; in the second, existence itself is a misery only to be endured until the welcome arrival of death the deliverer.[7]

Thus, Housman's emphasis on the value of death would seem, at least on a superficial examination, to cancel out the large number of poems which value life and living. It is necessary, therefore, to examine more closely Housman's treatment of death in *A Shropshire Lad* and to relate his view of death to the theme of the whole work.

Housman's obsession with death has been widely noted and condemned. R. P. Blackmur found that Housman wrote "almost entirely of death,"[8] and the notion that death is somehow central to the theme and mood of *A Shropshire Lad* is borne out by even a cursory reading of the work. Yet Housman's treatment of death has been subjected to frequent oversimplification and a rigidly literal interpretation. To be fully understood it must be seen in relation to the concern with permanence and change, innocence and experience, which lies at the heart of the work. Ignoring this relationship leads to the view that the poet's attitude toward death is capricious and inconsistent.

Since life is all too brief and death is the end of life, it would seem to follow that the poet would be opposed to death as the agent which destroys life; however, this is not always the case, for Housman's view of death in *A Shropshire Lad* takes a paradoxical turn. From the opening poem a world of change is established, and the quarrel with life in the lyrics of *A Shropshire Lad* lies in the realization that change and decay are the primary facts of existence. But *A Shropshire Lad* is also marked by a search for permanence in a world of change (in terms of the myth of the loss of innocence, the quest for the recovery of innocence after the Fall). The search for an agent to arrest the decay, to halt the flow of life and freeze life at its prime, leads to

[7] "The Poetry of A. E. Housman," *London Mercury,* VII (1922), 173.
[8] *The Expense of Greatness,* p. 202.

the conceit which is central to the work, a conceit in which death paradoxically becomes the only agent of stability in a life of ceaseless change.[9]

Housman's own life was marked by the same sort of quest that is mirrored in his poetry. On October 3, 1892, he delivered the traditional introductory lecture to open the academic year before the Faculties of Arts and Laws and Science in University College, London. He spoke of the value of learning and knowledge, and one passage is particularly revealing in indicating that his choice of a life of scholarship may have been related to the theme that underlies his poetry. He stated:

> The pleasures of the intellect are notoriously less vivid than either the pleasures of sense or the pleasures of the affections; and therefore, especially in the season of youth, the pursuit of knowledge is likely enough to be neglected and lightly esteemed in comparison with other pursuits offering much stronger immediate attractions. But the pleasure of learning and knowing, though not the keenest, is yet the least perishable of pleasures; the least subject to external things, and the play of chance, and the wear of time. And as a prudent man puts money by to serve as a provision for the material wants of his old age, so too he needs to lay up against the end of his days provision for the intellect. As the years go by, comparative values are found to alter: Time, says Sophocles, takes many things which once were

[9] The term *conceit* is most often defined in its narrower sense of an ingenious and elaborated comparison between unlike things. It is used here in the broader definition offered by Raymond M. Alden ("The Lyrical Conceit of the Elizabethans," *Studies in Philology*, XIV [1917], 129–52). Alden notes that some of the most interesting conceits of both the Petrarchan and metaphysical schools are not based on imagery. That is, they are not merely elaborated metaphors and similes but represent mental processes. These he classifies as "logical," as opposed to the more common "verbal" and "imaginative" conceits. Housman's use of the immortalizing virtue of death fits this classification, as does Keats's similar use of art, discussed later. In fact, Alden quotes from "Ode on a Grecian Urn" as an example of this type and states further that although we do not usually label such a poetic device as conceit, it represents a method "which we have found in Shakespeare and Sidney, and which we might find in poets of a certain type in any age" (p. 152).

pleasures and brings them nearer to pain. In the days when the strong men shall bow themselves, and desire shall fail, it will be a matter of yet more concern than now, whether one can say "my mind to me a kingdom is"; and whether the windows of the soul look out upon a broad and delightful landscape, or face nothing but a brick wall.[10]

Here is a link between Housman's scholarship and his poetry. Both represent a search for permanence in a mutable world. The unique virtue of learning for Housman is that it is not subject to the "wear of time." The world of scholarship exists apart, "the least subject to external things." How strongly the phenomenon of change affected Housman's thinking and writing is thus evident from the lecture delivered less than three years before the spring of 1895, when a large number of the poems of *A Shropshire Lad* were written. The quest for permanence, which is a part of the argument for the supremacy of the pleasures of the intellect over the pleasures of the senses in Housman's scholarly activities, becomes a molding idea in his poetry. It is in this context that his concern with death in *A Shropshire Lad* must be seen.

The complexity which characterizes Housman's view of death is nowhere seen more clearly than in Lyric XIX, "To an Athlete Dying Young." The athlete in the poem obviously symbolizes for the poet that period of greatest value in life, for he has both youth and achievement. Consequently, he is regarded as a "smart lad, to slip betimes away" from the ever fleeting phantom of life and into the permanence of death. "To an Athlete Dying Young" is thus one expression of the paradox which underlies *A Shropshire Lad*: death, the enemy of mankind, offers at times an occasion for joy.

The paradox that the poem develops is carefully reinforced through the poem's imagery. As Brooks and Warren have noted,[11] Housman uses the images which are associated with

10 *A. E. Housman: Selected Prose*, p. 20.
11 Cleanth Brooks and Robert Penn Warren, *Understanding Poetry* (New York, 1938), p. 385.

the youth's achievements to describe his death. Stanzas 1 and 2 of the poem describe the two triumphant processions in which the athlete has taken part. In the first he is carried triumphantly through the town on the shoulders of his friends after winning a race:

> The time you won your town the race
> We chaired you through the market-place;
> Man and boy stood cheering by,
> And home we brought you shoulder-high.
>
> (ll. 1–4)

In stanza 2 the young athlete is brought home dead, but the parallels between this procession and the former triumph are carefully drawn:

> To-day, the road all runners come,
> Shoulder-high we bring you home,
> And set you at your threshold down,
> Townsman of a stiller town.
>
> (ll. 5–8)

The implication of this parallel is that death, too, is a victory; but the youth is regarded as a "smart lad" not simply because he is dead but because his death has occurred at the prime of life. He will not have to watch his records being broken by other, more youthful men after his physical prowess has been withered by age:

> Eyes the shady night has shut
> Cannot see the record cut,
> And silence sounds no worse than cheers
> After earth has stopped the ears. . . .
>
> (ll. 13–16)

Thus death in the poem becomes the agent by which the process of change is halted. There is a sharp contrast between the mutability of the world of the living and the new-found permanence of the youth in death. In stanza 3 the physical world is identified as "fields where glory does not stay," and the poet adds that "early though the laurel grows / It withers quicker than the rose" (ll. 11–12). The laurel and the rose here apparently represent fame and beauty,[12] both subject to decay in life but not, according to the conceit of the poem, in death. In the last stanza the poet returns in an oblique way to the laurel and the rose, and he presses the contrast between life and death. He is describing the athlete in death:

> And round that early-laurelled head
> Will flock to gaze the strengthless dead,
> And find unwithered on its curls
> The garland briefer than a girl's.
>
> (ll. 25–28)

Here through the references to the "early-laurelled head" and the garland "briefer than a girl's" the poem suggests again the notions of fame and beauty, which were spoken of in stanza 3 as withering quickly in life. In death, however, the youth's garland is "unwithered on its curls." The poem thus emphasizes the contrast between two states, one marked by decay, the other by permanence.

Recognizing the relationship between Housman's view of death and his concern with mutability, one is led to the obvious conclusion that death in "To an Athlete Dying Young" is a part of a poetic conceit which runs throughout the poem. As a practical answer to the problem of change, the notion appears ridiculous; but of course it is the very nature of the conceit to bring together radically dissimilar ideas which are illogical to the common-sense world of fact. Keats's "Ode on a Grecian Urn," for example, uses a conceit similar to Housman's in conveying meaning which could be expressed effectively in no other way. The danger of abstracting Housman's view of death and discussing it literally as a philosophical belief thus becomes immediately apparent. This danger is illustrated by a comparison of Housman's "To an Athlete Dying Young" and Keats's "Ode on a Grecian Urn."

Parallels between the two poems are numerous. In both, life

12 See *ibid.*, p. 385.

has been frozen at the moment of highest intensity. Keats's urn is a "still unravish'd bride," and Housman's athlete in death holds high the "still-defended challenge-cup." In both poems there is a triumph over time. In Keats's poem the figures are frozen in action on an ancient urn, but because they can never consummate their actions, they are "for ever warm and still to be enjoyed / For every panting, and for ever young." Keats, too, contrasts this state of permanence in art with that of life. He finds that the passions frozen on the urn are

> All breathing human passion far above,
> That leaves a heart high-sorrowful and cloy'd,
> A burning forehead and a parching tongue.
> (ll. 28–39)

Housman's athlete is frozen in death also. In fact, the description of the dead youth serves to fix him in an immobile position in space and time:

> So set, before its echoes fade,
> The fleet foot on the sill of shade,
> And hold to the low lintel up
> The still-defended challenge-cup.
> (ll. 21–24)

Elizabeth Nitchie's attempt to find the source for this imagery offers a further parallel with Keats's poem, although she does not herself imply that such a parallel exists. She points out that carvings of some Greek stelae represent the dead person standing or sitting in a doorway. Such pictures, she finds, obviate the necessity of the interpretations of the "low lintel" of line 23 as the edge of the grave or as the lid of the coffin, as other critics have suggested.[13] Whether Housman had such carvings in mind, it is true that his description of the youth in the final stanza is almost that of a statue, around which the dead gather ("And round that early-laurelled head / Will flock to gaze the strengthless dead").

13 "Housman's 'To an Athlete Dying Young,' " *Explicator*, X (1951–52), Item 31.

Both poems, then, are constructed around a poetic conceit which is meaningful only in the context of the poem. Housman uses a certain metaphorical conception of death in the same way that Keats uses the conception of art—to halt the decay of time and preserve the moment of highest intensity. To abstract either conception from the poem is to destroy it by ignoring its context, a principle so necessary to the integrity of the poem as a whole that it must not be overlooked. It is also important to recognize that this conceit runs through a number of the poems of *A Shropshire Lad.*

Lyric XII, "When I Watch the Living Meet," illustrates a similar conception of death as a metaphorical agent for halting decay. Again, the poem contrasts the two states of being and nonbeing. Life is characterized as "the house of flesh" where "the heats of hate and lust / . . . are strong." Death is the "house of dust" where "revenges are forgot, / And the hater hates no more." The two states are contrasted also in time of duration. In life man will "lodge a little while," but in the house of dust, his "sojourn shall be long." The last stanza of the poem again recalls Keats's ode as its depicts two lovers in death:

> Lovers lying two and two
> Ask not whom they sleep beside,
> And the bridegroom all night through
> Never turns him to the bride.
> (ll. 13–16)

In death the lovers are forever bride and bridegroom. Their state can never be altered by time. It is thus regarded as superior to the "house of flesh," characterized by "the heats of hate and lust." Death has caught the lovers at the highest point of their love and halted the progression of time.

Lyric XLIII, "The Immortal Part," as its title suggests, further displays Housman's search for permanence. Here the tone is frankly ironic, for the poem's theme is that only the bones of man survive death, emphasizing the vanity of the world of flesh. In stanza 2 the bones, "the immortal part," ask:

"When shall this slough of sense be cast,
This dust of thoughts be laid at last,
The man of flesh and soul be slain
And the man of bone remain?"

(ll. 5–8)

The permanent man, the man of bone, is born only after the temporal man of flesh and mind has melted away. Immortality, the object of man's quest, is achieved, but it is a bitter victory:

"The immortal bones obey control
Of dying flesh and dying soul.

" 'Tis long till eve and morn are gone:
Slow the endless night comes on,
And late to fulness grows the birth
That shall last as long as earth."

(ll. 15–20)

In "The Immortal Part" the images associated with life are temporal objects—fire, smoke, and dust—and the flesh is seen merely as an empty vessel or a garment which is worn by the skeleton, which in death achieves its mastery because it alone is immortal.

Lyric XVI is interesting in depicting in one image both the transitory nature of life and the permanence found in death. The entire poem is devoted to the description of a scene in which a nettle is tossed about on a grave by the wind:

It nods and curtseys and recovers
When the wind blows above,
The nettle on the graves of lovers
That hanged themselves for love.

The nettle nods, the wind blows over,
The man, he does not move,
The lover of the grave, the lover
That hanged himself for love.

One notes, first of all, that the contrast in the poem's imagery is in terms of motion and rest. The nettle "nods and curtseys and recovers," but the man, "he does not move." Randall Jarrell, in discussing the poem, equates the nettle with living man, the wind with the force of life:

> The nettle is merely repeating above the grave, compelled by the wind, what the man in the grave did once, when the wind blew through him. So living is (we must take it as being) just a repetition of little meaningless nodding actions, actions that haven't even the virtue of being our own—since the wind forces them out of us; life as the wind makes man as the tree or nettle helpless and determined.[14]

It is not necessary, however, to view the poem in the fatalistic light which Jarrell's reading suggests. Housman is able, through the symbols of the nettle, the wind, and the dead lover, to draw a complex image of life's transitory state—complex, as Jarrell himself states, because grass, which is a common symbol for transitoriness, here outlasts man and serves, in addition, to reinforce the notion of man's mutable state. The nettle is clearly a symbol of the state of human existence; but the paradox of the poem is that the "lover of the grave" has triumphed over the forces of life symbolized by the nettle and the wind, for he has escaped the ceaseless cycle of change which the nettle must continually undergo as it is buffeted by the wind. The ambiguity of line 7 now becomes more crucial. At first the reader assumes that he is to regard the lover in the poem in the conventional sense—that is, he hanged himself for love of a woman. Yet line 7 identifies the lover as "the lover of the grave." This may be read in two ways: the lover who now lies in the grave or the man who loves the grave. The first meaning is more obvious, but both apply. The nettle, symbolic of the hurtful nature of man's existence, is characterized as being thrown into an endless cycle by the wind, or life force (a cyclical pattern being suggested by the series of motion—*nods, curtseys, recovers*). The lover, however, has escaped this cycle: "he does not move." He was able to exchange the transitory nature of

14 "Texts from Housman," *Kenyon Review,* I (1939), 267.

life for the permanence achieved only in death because he was, as the second meaning of line 7 implies, a "lover of the grave" and "hanged himself for love" [of the grave]. He has escaped the "fields where glory does not stay" in the same way as the youth of "To an Athlete Dying Young."

The recognition of the oblique presence of this death conceit has the effect of complicating poems which have always been regarded as the epitome of simplicity and directness, as seen in one of the most popular of the lyrics of *A Shropshire Lad*, Lyric LIV:

> With rue my heart is laden
>   For golden friends I had,
> For many a rose-lipt maiden
>   And many a lightfoot lad.
>
> By brooks too broad for leaping
>   The lightfoot boys are laid;
> The rose-lipt girls are sleeping
>   In fields where roses fade.

The poem illustrates Housman's ability to depict a commonplace emotion with great complexity. He is dealing with the sense of loss one feels for the dead, yet in creating this emotion he manages to suggest both the idea of life's loss through change and the idea of death's victory over this loss. This suggestion does not occur in the thought of the poem, which is straightforward enough, contained essentially in the first two lines, but in the pattern of its imagery.

John Crowe Ransom has objected to the first line of the poem as "painful, grandiloquent, incredible to the naturalistic imagination." He states further,

> . . . I think we must have misgivings as to the propriety of linking this degree of desolation with the loss of friends in wholesale quantities. Grief is not exactly cumulative, not proportionate to the numerical occasions; it is the quality of a single grief rather than the total quantity of all the

griefs that we expect to be developed in a poem, if the poem is in the interest of the deepest possible sentiment.[15]

True enough, yet the poem is not at all concerned with any specific death; it is an analysis of the consciousness of death and of the effect of this awareness on the narrator. The poem, after all, begins with emphasis on the narrator's thoughts: "With rue my heart is laden. . . ." Ransom's quibble with *laden* in line 1 also misses the irony inherent in the imagery of the poem. The poem depicts the emotion of the narrator in paradoxical terms, which, in turn, parallels the larger paradox developed in the poem. The sense of desolation, or emptiness, is produced by *laden,* suggesting fullness. The sense of stillness in lines 5 and 6 is depicted by *leaping,* and the impression of rosiness in lines 7 and 8 is suggested by reference to the fading of roses. The poem has thus managed to produce through this imagery simultaneously the stillness of death and the activity of life.

The image of "golden friends" in line 2 also contributes to the paradoxical theme of the poem. Although Ransom objects that "the image needs a little specification: Shakespeare's golden lads and girls were in better order by virtue of the contrasts with the chimney-sweepers,"[16] the absence of explicit color contrast may in fact help the image to perform its function. In both works, *golden* must be taken in its classical (Golden Age) and physical sense. Just as in alchemy gold represented the perfect mixture of the elements, the lads and girls of Shakespeare's and Housman's lyrics represent the time in which the elements of life are in perfect harmony. In Shakespeare's imagery this gold is turned to dust by time ("Golden lads and girls all must, / As chimney-sweepers, come to dust") ; yet the point which has eluded critics of Housman's poem is that, strictly in terms of the imagery of the poem, the golden friends

15 "Honey and Gall," *Southern Review,* VI (1940) , 7.
16 *Ibid.*

escape the decay of time. Housman manages this by transferring the sense of change from the dead youths to the physical world from which they have escaped. The "lightfoot lad" of line 4 is still described as lightfoot in death; however, the brooks he was accustomed to leap in youth are now "too broad for leaping." Likewise, the "rose-lipt maiden" maintains, in the poem's imagery, the complexion of her youth; yet she is sleeping in "fields where roses fade." Housman thus continues the conceit in which death becomes the agent for halting time, for fixing and maintaining the moment in which life is golden. Change is a property of the living, not of the dead.

Ransom further objects that Housman does not depict strikingly enough the shameful end which death involves. He states, referring to the rose-lipt girls:

> . . . that does not seem too shameful an end. Roses fade in the best of fields. . . . What we require is an image to carry the fading of the rosy lips; to be buried in the ground involves this disgrace sufficiently for brutal logic but not for poetic imagination.[17]

Ransom's statement serves to point up the danger of ignoring the unity of theme in *A Shropshire Lad*. If the reader is conscious of the continuing conceit Housman constructs about death in the work, he realizes that the poem scrupulously avoids the suggestion that death brings with it a decay, and, instead, emphasizes the decay that characterizes life. Housman's seemingly simple statement about death, which Ransom finds inept, becomes somewhat more complex on closer examination, for the attitude toward death in the poem is a complex one. Stanza 1 offers only an overwhelming sense of grief; yet this feeling of loss is altered in stanza 2 by the deeper insight that death is both a loss and a gain. But this is a complexity which must be seen, finally, in the whole of *A Shropshire Lad,* and critics who consider only isolated poems may conclude, like Ransom, that

17 *Ibid.,* p. 8.

the ironical detail of this poem is therefore fairly inept. The imagination of this poet is not a trained and faithful instrument, or at least it does not work well for him here. That is not an additional charge, however, to saying that the poem as a whole is not very satisfactory, for it is the specific ground of the poem's failure. There cannot be a fine poetry without a fine poetic texture.[18]

But Ransom's judgment of the poem is weakened by his lack of attention to the theme of the work of which the poem is a part. He condemns the poem for failing to make death shameful enough without realizing that to have done so would have violated the continuity of the theme of *A Shropshire Lad.* And even though the theme is not directly stated in Lyric LIV (although it is certainly present), elsewhere in the work it receives more direct treatment. Lyric XXIII, for example, helps strengthen the interpretation of Lyric LIV as a poem which regards death not wholly as a shameful end. The scene of Lyric XXIII is Ludlow Fair. The narrator watches the hundreds of lads as they arrive from "the barn and the forge and the mill and the fold. . . ." He sees that some are there for the girls and some for the liquor, but his interest lies in another group, for "there with the rest are the lads that will never be old" (l. 4). It is in the contrast between the first two groups and the last that the heart of the poem lies. Many of the first group are, in their prime, handsome and brave:

> And many to count are the stalwart, and many the brave,
> And many the handsome of face and the handsome of heart,
>   And few that will carry their looks or their truth to the grave.
> (ll. 6–8)

The latter group, however, are regarded as "fortunate fellows" (compare this with the "smart lad" of Lyric XIX), for they will "carry back bright to the coiner the mintage of man" (l. 15). The last line of the poem makes clear why these men

18 *Ibid.*

are to be regarded as fortunate, and how they are to preserve the "mintage of man"; these are "the lads that will die in their glory and never be old" (l. 16).

Again, it would be easy to oversimplify the attitude toward death in this poem and regard death merely as an escape from the misery of existence, as many of Housman's critics have insisted. But, viewing the poem in relation to the theme of the whole work, one must conclude that here, as elsewhere in *A Shropshire Lad,* the point is not that these lads have escaped some sort of evil inherent in all of life, but that they, instead, have escaped the change and decay of time; and as Housman's coin image suggests, they have preserved something which in itself is valuable.

Lyric XLIV deals with yet another aspect of life's mutability, the sudden change of fortune with which living man is powerless to contend. Here, even the act of suicide becomes an acceptable means of defeating fate by stopping time:

> Shot? so quick, so clean an ending?
>   Oh that was right, lad, that was brave:
> Yours was not an ill for mending,
>   'Twas best to take it to the grave.
>
> Oh you had forethought, you could reason,
>   And saw your road and where it led,
> And early wise and brave in season
>   Put the pistol to your head.
>
> (ll. 1–8)

Suicide thus becomes justified because, even though death is not desirable, the ills of time and the disgraces of ever changing fortune are even less desirable: "Dust's your wages, son of sorrow, / But men may come to worse than dust" (ll. 15–16). Stanzas 5 and 6 of the poem make clear that, again, death is not regarded merely as escape from the evil and injustice of the world. It is, instead, a means to "carry back bright to the coiner the mintage of man." Man is considered here in generic terms. By his act of suicide the lad has saved himself and his fellow men the dishonor and guilt which his unnamed disgrace would have brought them:

> Souls undone, undoing others, —
>   Long time since the tale began.
> You would not live to wrong your brothers:
>   O lad, you died as fits a man.
>
> Now to your grave shall friend and stranger
>   With ruth and some with envy come:
> Undishonored, clear of danger,
>   Clean of guilt, pass hence and home.
>
>   (ll. 17–24)

The source of the poem casts some further light on these lines. Laurence Housman writes in his biography of his brother:

> On August 6th, 1895, a young Woolwich Cadet, aged eighteen, took his own life, leaving a long letter addressed to the Coroner to say why he had done so. The gist of that letter was quoted in a newspaper cutting of the day, which I found lying in my brother's copy of *A Shropshire Lad* alongside the poem which begins:
>   Shot? so quick, so clean an ending?
> It is quite evident that certain passages in that letter prompted the writing of the poem; one sentence indeed is almost quoted.[19]

Laurence Housman then quotes a part of the young Cadet's letter:

> "I wish it to be clearly understood that I am not what is commonly called 'temporarily insane' and that I am putting an end to my life after several weeks of careful deliberation. I do not think that I need to justify my actions to anyone but my Maker, but . . . I will state the main reasons which have determined me. The first is utter cowardice and despair. There is only one thing in this world which would make me thoroughly happy; that one thing I have no earthly hope of obtaining. The second—which I

19 *My Brother, A. E. Housman* (New York, 1938), pp. 103–104.

wish was the only one—is that I have absolutely ruined my own life; but I thank God that as yet, so far as I know, I have not morally injured, or 'offended,' as it is called in the Bible, anyone else. Now I am quite certain that I could not live another five years without doing so, and for that reason alone, even if the first did not exist, I should do what I am doing. . . . At all events it is final, and consequently better than a long series of sorrows and disgraces."[20]

The last two sentences quoted above must certainly have attracted Housman to the story, for they parallel the concept of death which recurs throughout the poems written during this period. The young man died to halt the moral decay which is mentioned in the letter ("I could not live another five years without doing so, . . ."). Housman applauds this idea in lines 19 and 20: "You would not live to wrong your brothers: / O lad, you died as fits a man." The last sentence quoted from the letter contains the idea which forms the basis of the concept of death stated most clearly in "To an Athlete Dying Young." The young Cadet wrote, "At all events it is final, and consequently better than a long series of sorrows and disgraces." Compare Housman's lines: "Oh soon, and better so than later / After long disgrace and scorn, . . ." (ll. 9–10) .

The Cadet parallels the "smart lad" and the "fortunate fellows" in escaping the ill fortunes of time. The last stanza of the poem offers him still further compensations:

> Turn safe to rest, no dreams, no waking;
> And here, man, here's the wreath I've made:
> 'Tis not a gift that's worth the taking,
> But wear it and it will not fade.

(ll. 25–28)

The wreath mentioned in line 26 may be identified on two levels. On the literal level it is the token of victory, the poet's sign that the lad has triumphed over the adversities of time. It will not fade because it is artificial, not organic ("a wreath

20 *Ibid.,* p. 104.

I've made"). It may be compared to the garland which the athlete's head bears "unwithered on its curls." But the wreath may also be interpreted as the poem itself (an artifact which is made and, again, because it is artificial, not subject to the wear of time). The poet thus offers the lad the permanence of art, repeating the conceit of Shakespeare's Sonnet 18. Both poets recognize the mutability of the natural world, where "every fair from fair sometime declines, / By chance or nature's changing course untrimmed." (Sonnet 18, ll. 7–8), and both offer the permanence of art to halt the decay. Shakespeare argues that through his poem "thy eternal summer shall not fade" (l. 9); Housman's statement is remarkably close: "But wear it and it will not fade."

Perhaps it is not necessary to point out that both death and art are utilized in much the same manner by Housman in this poem and in other lyrics of *A Shropshire Lad,* as poetic answers to the dilemma posed by an awareness of the mutable nature of man's existence. Yet apparently numerous critics have ignored this aspect of Housman's view of death in the work. Their error lies in confusing poetic conceit and philosophical belief. No critic has been naïve enough to assume that Shakespeare believed his poem would literally preserve the beauty of the young man to whom Sonnet 18 is addressed. Yet Housman's use of a similar conceit has been interpreted literally with the resulting judgment that his philosophy is perverse and contradictory.

A Shropshire Lad is centered on the human dilemma of life and death, mutability and permanence, and this dilemma can be resolved only in paradoxical terms. Cleanth Brooks, in *The Well Wrought Urn,* has argued for the necessity of the statement of paradox:

> If the poet . . . must perforce dramatize the oneness of the experience, even through paying tribute to its diversity, then his use of paradox and ambiguity is seen as necessary. He is not simply trying to spice up, with a superficially exciting or mystifying rhetoric, the old stale stockpot. . . .

He is rather giving us an insight which preserves the unity of experience and which at its higher and more serious levels, triumphs over the apparently contradictory and conflicting elements of experience by unifying them into a new pattern.[21]

It is in this sense that Housman's paradoxical view of death must be regarded. As a practical answer to the dilemma posed by time, Housman's poetry ultimately fails. But the lyric poet, it must be agreed, has traditionally not attempted to provide practical answers to life's problems, and his poetic answers serve only as occasional insights into the human condition.

In his own terms, in the framework of his poetry, the pattern which Housman imposes on the flux of experience is consistent. But this is a unity of pattern which must be viewed in the whole work. It is, of course, not a strictly logical unity in the sense that one lyric leads logically to another (even though, as may be seen later, the arrangement of the poems is meaningful); it is instead what Brooks has called "the unification of attitude." He states:

The characteristic unity of a poem (even of those poems which may accidentally possess a logical unity as well as this poetic unity) lies in the unification of attitudes into a hierarchy subordinated to a total and governing attitude. In the unified poem, the poet has "come to terms" with his experience. The conclusion of the poem is the working out of the various tensions set up by whatever means—by propositions, metaphors, symbols. The unity is achieved by a dramatic process, not a logical; it represents an equilibrium of forces, not a formula. It is "proved" as a dramatic conclusion is proved: by its ability to resolve the conflicts which have been accepted as the *données* of the drama.[22]

He concludes:

. . . it is easy to see why the relation of each item of the whole

[21] *Brooks*, pp. 213–14.
[22] *Ibid.*, pp. 206–207.

context is crucial, and why the effective and essential structure of the poem has to do with the complex of attitudes achieved. A scientific proposition can stand alone. If it is true, it is true. But the expression of an attitude, apart from the occasion which generates it and the situation which it encompasses, is meaningless.[23]

It seems clear that a thematic unity pervades *A Shropshire Lad*. Yet if it is to be regarded as having the unity almost of a single poem, there remains the matter of the relationship of each part to the whole. In the discussion of theme it has been necessary to examine the lyrics separately, taking them out of their structural context. But the unity of the whole depends finally upon the arrangement of its separate parts, in this case the sixty-three lyrics which make up *A Shropshire Lad*.

23 *Ibid.*, p. 207.

IV

THE STRUCTURE OF *A SHROPSHIRE LAD*

*I*n 1966 the whole question of the ordering of the poems of *A Shropshire Lad* was reopened with the publication of Tom Burns Haber's manuscript variorum, *The Making of A Shropshire Lad*. Haber's objective was to provide "a new and broader comprehension of Housman's development";[1] his method, to examine the notebooks now in The Library of Congress which contain early drafts of the lyrics of *A Shropshire Lad,* and to print these drafts in the various stages of their development. One of the problems Haber was forced to consider was the order of the poems. Did Housman, in fact, arrange the sixty-three lyrics in some thematic sequence? Haber concludes that he did not. His reasons for this conclusion and the arguments of some earlier critics in favor of a thematic arrangement provide a necessary prologue to the present examination of the design of the work as a whole.

Haber mentions only two critics who have suggested that *A Shropshire Lad* is an ordered sequence of poems, Ian Scott-Kilvert and Nesca A. Robb, but there have been others. One of Housman's earliest reviewers, Richard Le Gallienne, noted in 1896, shortly after the publication of the work, that the sixty-three lyrics of *A Shropshire Lad* must be studied as a whole. Yet in supporting this view he offered nothing more specific than the statement that "a character is self-revealed and a story is told, with here and there glimpses of a comrade and his story . . . all having a certain personal bearing, all contributing

[1] *The Making of A Shropshire Lad* (Seattle, 1966) , p. 3.

to paint the picture of the 'Shropshire Lad's' world and its ways. . . ."[2] The more recent statement of Ian Scott-Kilvert on the work's order is equally vague. He finds that the poems "are grouped in the manner of a sonnet-sequence, introducing and contrasting a succession of themes so balanced that none should overweigh the others."[3] He fails, however, to go beyond this assertion with any detailed examination of the poems, and his contention that the poems have the unity of a sonnet-sequence had been earlier rejected by J. B. Priestley, who stated:

> The poems are not, as it were, threaded on a string . . . they have not that sort of unity, that dependence upon one another, which we usually find in—say—a sonnet-sequence; but nevertheless one spirit breathes through them; they flow out of one central mood.[4]

Yet Priestley himself suggested some sort of orderly arrangement of the poems:

> . . . what Housman did in this volume was to depart from the usual practice of our modern lyric poets: instead of directly expressing his various moods he partly dramatised them in a more or less definite atmosphere, on a more or less consistent plan.[5]

Priestley did not say what this plan was, but he did suggest that its discovery would be quite valuable in any interpretation of Housman's poetry: "In any long study it would certainly be worth while examining the poems and trying to decide what the poet has gained by adopting so unusual a plan, gained, that is, not in this poem or that, but in the whole mass regarded as a complete and distinct work."[6]

Only one critic, Nesca A. Robb, has attempted to deal with the structure of the work on the scope suggested by Priestley,

---

2 Quoted in Richards, p. 7.
3 *A. E. Housman*, p. 24.
4 "The Poetry of A. E. Housman," *London Mercury*, VII (1922), 173.
5 *Ibid.*, p. 176.
6 *Ibid.*, p. 177.

and her statement of the unity of *A Shropshire Lad* is the strongest and most explicit that has yet appeared:

> *A Shropshire Lad* is an ordered sequence. One might almost go farther and call it a poem, for the more one studies it the more intimately do its component parts appear to be related to one another. They are arranged with deliberateness, so that not only does one theme follow another in logical sequence, but the themes prophesy, recall and intertwine with each other so that, as one grows familiar with the whole, one comes to feel the closest organic connection between the individual poems.[7]

Unfortunately, Miss Robb's method of dealing with the work's structure is sometimes more impressionistic than critical. She states, for example, in supporting her view that the work is an ordered sequence:

> The feelings expressed in *The Immortal Part* (No. XLIII) add a new content to the phrase "the lover of the grave" in No. XVI. The exile's dream of the "high snowdrifts" on the hawthorns of his native shire recalls inevitably "the cherry hung with snow" and makes one feel more strongly what a capacity for pain is already implicit and stirring in the poet's delight. The casual lovemaking of "Oh, see how thick the gold cup flowers" emphasizes the gulf of human experience that lies between the lighthearted falsehood and the tortured sincerity of "If truth in hearts that perish."[8]

What she has noted here is a thematic unity; the examples she draws from the work do not support a meaningful order among the poems. If "The Immortal Part" (No. XLIII) had preceded No. XVI, one could still make the same statement about the relationship between the two poems. The same may be said of two of her other examples. "Oh, see how thick the gold cup flowers" and "If truth in hearts that perish" emphasize "the gulf of human experience that lies between the lighthearted

7 "A. E. Housman" in *Four in Exile* (London, 1948), p. 12.
8 *Ibid.*

falsehood and the tortured sincerity" no matter in what order they appear in the work. Miss Robb does find, however, a logical sequence in the work, especially in the narrative element devoted to the Shropshire lad himself. Her method is to relate each of the early poems to the lad's emotional development. The first poem represents "a celebration of present friendship and of the valour and delight of young manhood"; the second reveals the moment when youth "first grows aware of the lapse of hours, and instinctively reaches out to clasp life's joys more closely." In the next poem, "the young man is called to seek the military glory that has dignified his fellows," and in "Reveille," No. IV, he is bidden to "cast off sloth and taste all the experiences he may while the day lasts."[9] She follows this method up to Lyric IX, where she is forced to drop a poem-by-poem analysis because of apparently irrelevant material which fails to conform to her scheme. The remainder of her discussion is from a thematic point of view, by which she finds certain groupings of themes: poems about murderers, for example, poems about exile, and poems about young lovers.

Because Miss Robb failed to demonstrate conclusively anything more than a unity of tone and mood, her conclusions on the ordering of the poems have not been influential. George Watson, dealing with the arrangement of the poems in one of the latest biographies of Housman, ignores her findings completely, stating that the principle by which Housman selected the sequence of poems from the notebooks is "more judicious than meaningful." Watson feels that Housman's guiding principle was "the omission of any material that might betray to the world at large some oblique biographical reference."[10] Haber dismisses her, along with Scott-Kilvert, in a footnote. Obviously, he did not feel compelled to refute these critics at any great length because of their failure, on the whole, to demonstrate convincingly that any meaningful arrangement exists.

[9] *Ibid.*, pp. 18–19.
[10] *A. E. Housman: A Divided Life,* p. 158.

Haber's own conclusion is that "it is the charm and force of the individual poems in *A Shropshire Lad,* taken in sum, not thematic movements, that constitute the appeal of the book. Such problems as order and climax, the building up of tonal effects, nuance, and resolution did not present themselves significantly to Housman." In short, he can find "little objective evidence of thematic design in *A Shropshire Lad.*"[11]

Haber offers only two bits of evidence gleaned from the notebooks to support his conclusion. He feels that two of the opening poems, "1887" and "The Recruit," are a vestige of the "catch-penny design" of his publisher to make the book a "romance of enlistment."[12] But he adds:

> More important than theme sequence, I believe, is his confidence in the twelve pieces he chose to follow the five assigned to the vanguard. Looking again at these five pieces, we see that the military tone of "1887" and "The Recruit" is supported by at least the title of "Reveille" (ASL 4) even though the poem itself is not in praise of redcoats; "Loveliest of trees . . ." (ASL 2) is a lesson learned from nature, and "Oh see how thick the goldcup flowers" (ASL 5) is an idyll of casual lovemaking. This quintet sounds the keynote of *A Shropshire Lad*: the poems remind us of youth and its swift passing, its pleasures, duties, and inevitable defeats. But Housman's selection of the next twelve poems was guided by quite a different principle, which emerges from the fact that all of these pieces are

11 Haber, *The Making of A Shropshire Lad*, pp. 22–23. In *A. E. Housman* (New York, 1967), written for Twayne's English Authors Series, Haber repeats his contention that Housman did not introduce any broad sequential patterns in *A Shropshire Lad*: "After a careful summing-up of the question of sequence and design, I conclude that, rather than making thematic patterns of his poems—which would tend to subordinate and tone them down—Housman deliberately, for the most part, set his *Shropshire Lad* pieces against each other" (pp. 94–95).

12 Haber, *The Making of A Shropshire Lad*, p. 21. Laurence Housman reprints a letter from his brother in which he spoke of this plan and his refusal to pursue it. Laurence notes that his brother regarded patriotism as a dangerous subject for poets (*My Brother, A. E. Housman*, p. 83).

represented in the notebooks by unique drafts. Some of these were written early—number 14 ("There pass the careless people") is the second *Shropshire Lad* lyric in Notebook A and dates from before 1890. Others of the twelve came late—number 6 ("When the lad for longing sighs") belongs to the autumn of 1895. The notebook drafts of two or three of the others in this group make hard reading now, and some recopies were probably made outside the notebooks, but the important fact is that ASL 6 to 17 existed there in the form of single drafts only. The inspiration of walks that produced them achieved in the very first transcription a finality that made them worthy of being written into printer's copy.[13]

Haber's attempt to account for the presence of twelve of the first seventeen poems by the fact that they were in a relatively finished state (he infers this from the fact that they are represented in the notebooks by only one draft) ignores his own findings that over thirty poems, not just twelve, are found in the same state in the notebooks. Eighteen such poems represented by unique drafts come much later in the final arrangement (three of the last five poems, for example) . Furthermore, many of these appear quite early in the notebooks. If Housman's basis for selecting the opening poems for the printer's copy was merely the fact that the poems were in a finished state, then it is strange that he overlooked the other eighteen poems, reserving them for the middle and concluding portions of the book. Haber's explanation, based on the presence of unique drafts in the manuscript, certainly offers no satisfactory basis for the final arrangement of the poems.

He also points to the changes made after the printer's copy had been prepared as evidence that Housman had no thematic arrangement in mind. Housman withdrew five poems and added three while the book was in the hands of the printer. Haber has discovered also that he made fourteen changes in numerals,

[13] Haber, *The Making of A Shropshire Lad*, p. 21.

seven of which were again altered in the proofsheets, and concludes from this that "even if Housman had cherished the idea
of a definite thematic system . . . he probably would have been
obliged to abandon it" in the light of these changes.[14] This is
a curious argument indeed, for the changes made would suggest, to the contrary, that the ordering was significant to Housman, and, in fact, as will be shown later, the alterations made
in the printer's copy tend to support rather than to disprove
the notion that *A Shropshire Lad* is constructed around a thematic movement which is carefully preserved in the final arrangement of the poems. Haber also fails to take into account
the evidence *for* a schematic arrangement—the fact that Housman refused to allow poems from *A Shropshire Lad* (but not
Last Poems) to be taken out of context and included in anthologies, and the even more curious fact that he prohibited
the publication of poems from *A Shropshire Lad* and *Last
Poems* together in one volume, all of which led his second
publisher, Grant Richards, to the opinion that the poet probably regarded the book as a sequence of poems not to be altered.[15]

It is, however, in the finished work itself that the final answer must be sought. The evidence derived from the manuscripts and the history of publication is secondary to the testi-
mony offered by the work as it stands in its completed form. It
is only after a close examination of the work as a whole that
one understands how some critics, while obviously believing
that the poems constitute a whole, have found it difficult to
articulate their reasons, for it is not in the specific relationship
of each lyric to every other but in the general movement
throughout the sixty-three poems that the complex theme of
A Shropshire Lad is embodied. The key to its over-all structure
is found in the underlying theme itself—the concern with the
loss of innocence, the discovery of a world of change and death,

14 *Ibid.*, p. 22.
15 Richards, p. 53.

and the quest for permanence. The archetypal expression of this theme is seen most clearly in the Eden myth and in the pastoral elegy, both of which are in evidence in the individual poems of *A Shropshire Lad*. The most essential element of both manifestations of lost innocence is the departure from the land of innocence, the Biblical Eden and the pastoral Arcadia. Poems such as "Loveliest of Trees" (No. II) and "Farewell to barn and stack and tree" (No. VIII) reveal Housman's use of both the underlying myth and the pastoral mode of its expression. The transition from a perception of life characterized by permanence to one marked by change, furthermore, forms the basis for the structure of the majority of the poems of *A Shropshire Lad*. It is in this context also that the larger pattern of the work takes shape.

If *A Shropshire Lad* is regarded as a whole, not simply a collection of poems, one discovers a remarkably consistent pattern of development. The first discovery which encourages even closer scrutiny is that the work contains a framework which gives meaning to the poems contained within. The first lyric and the last two not only serve as the poet's apologia but also provide the context in which the remaining sixty poems are illumined. It has perhaps been recognized that in the two concluding lyrics the poet justifies both the theme and the tone of the preceding poems; but the subtle relationship between the apologia and "1887," the poem which introduces the reader to the world of Shropshire, has been overlooked. An equally important point which has been ignored is that the lyrics which remain to form the body of the work are divided almost equally into two groups of poems: the first set in Shropshire; the second, outside Shropshire, principally in London. In between is the journey of exile that embodies the myth which lies at the core of Housman's art.

The general scheme of the work may thus be seen, somewhat oversimplified, by grouping the sixty-three lyrics into three divisions: the first (composed of Lyrics I, LXII, and LXIII), constituting a framing device; the second (composed of Lyrics II–XXXVII), set in Shropshire; the third (composed of Lyrics XXXVIII–LXI), the exile poems. Although this grouping is somewhat arbitrary—the dividing lines could perhaps be established at other places—it does provide a means by which the poems can be examined in some sequence, and ultimately, a means by which the design of the work can be demonstrated.

V

THE FRAME POEMS

A *Shropshire Lad* opens and closes with quite subtle allusions to other expressions of the theme it explores, principally Milton's *Paradise Lost* and Christ's parable of the sower of seeds. These allusions, which encourage an examination of the relationship between Housman's poems and the works they echo, support the belief that the position of the frame poems is deliberate. One may say with near certainty that Housman saw "1887" as an introductory poem and "Terence, This Is Stupid Stuff" (No. LXII) and "I Hoed and Trenched and Weeded" (No. LXIII) as his apologia. Further, one must conclude that Housman used these three poems to provide a context which illumines and clarifies the theme of his poetry, a conclusion which can be demonstrated by an analysis of the three frame poems, with special reference to their technique of allusion.

The appropriateness of "1887" as the introductory poem of the volume has been noted. It is the one poem of the work that makes specific reference to historical time and place—England in 1887, the year of the Golden Jubilee. The work begins by contrasting the mood of optimism which characterized England in the 1880's with the more somber reflections of one who is unable to share that faith. But more significant than this rather obvious prefatory element is the fact that the poem draws parallels between the celebration of the Golden Jubilee and another celebration, that of the fallen angels in Milton's *Paradise Lost.*

Immediately after the great consultation in Hell in Book II

of *Paradise Lost,* the fallen angels entertain themselves with an angelic version of the Olympic games, lighting up the sky with mock battles:

> As when, to warn proud cities, war appears
> Waged in the troubled sky, and armies rush
> To battle in the clouds; before each van
> Prick forth the airy knights, and couch their spears
> Till thickest legions close; with feats of arms
> From either end of Heaven the welkin burns.
>
> (ll. 533–38)[1]

The first line of "1887," which describes the sky illumined by the fires which honor Victoria's fiftieth year of reign, echoes line 538 of Milton's passage:

> From Clee to heaven the beacon burns,
> The shires have seen it plain,
> From north and south the sign returns
> And beacons burn again.
>
> (ll. 1–4)

"From either end of Heaven the welkin burns" becomes "From Clee to Heaven the beacon burns" with the dropping of the second foot, the substitution of *to* for *of* and *Clee* for *ei[ther], beacon* for *welkin.* In both significant changes, Housman's substitutions echo the sounds of Milton's words. The lines are so close in every detail that one must conclude that Housman was recalling the passage in *Paradise Lost.*

The contexts of both passages support this conclusion and suggest Housman's motive for opening *A Shropshire Lad* with an allusion to *Paradise Lost.* The crux of "1887" is located in the contrast between the attitudes of those who sing "God save the Queen" and one who, in the midst of this celebration, remembers "friends of ours / Who shared the work with God," the soldiers who now lie dead in foreign fields as victims of Fate. The persona imagines that the soldiers join the singing:

---

[1] *The Complete Poetical Works of John Milton,* ed. by Douglas Bush (Boston, 1965). All quotations from *Paradise Lost* are from this edition.

> "God save the Queen" we living sing,
>   From height to height 'tis heard;
> And with the rest your voices ring,
>   Lads of the Fifty-third.
>   (ll. 25–28)

In *Paradise Lost,* in the midst of the celebration of the war games, occur these lines:

> Others more mild,
> Retreated in a silent valley, sing
> With notes angelical to many a harp
> Their own heroic deeds and hapless fall
> By doom of battle; and complain that Fate
> Free Virtue should enthrall to Force or Chance.
>   (II, 546–51)

Here the same contrast is evident between those who celebrate war and those who acknowledge its cost. But one further passage from Book II, some seventy lines later, strengthens the parallel between the two works and perhaps explains why Housman was drawn to this section of *Paradise Lost.* Milton, in narrating the fallen angels' exploration of their new world, describes their discovery of

> A universe of death, which God by curse
> Created evil, for evil only good,
> Where all life dies, death lives. . . .
>   (II, 622–24)

It is just such a universe to which the Shropshire lad awakens in the poems immediately following "1887."

The parallels between the two works, which Housman's allusion points up, are thus quite revealing, for they provide a new perspective from which to view *A Shropshire Lad.* Housman's poetry, rather than being merely the product of a perverse reaction to a hostile world, as the weight of critical opinion would suggest, appears to belong in the tradition of English poetry that has attempted to justify, or at least come to terms with, the human situation. It would perhaps be too much to say that Housman is attempting to justify the ways of God to men; God is left almost entirely out of the picture. Yet on a less lofty scale, Housman is attempting a task similar to that which Milton set for himself. Both poets are concerned with the loss of the paradise of innocence, be it Eden or Shropshire. Both accept the archetype most central to this loss of innocence, and both employ the pastoral tradition in attempting to account for man's transition from a simple, "good" life to one marked by guilt and death.[2] The body of *A Shropshire Lad* (Lyrics II–LXI) develops this theme and its implications, and the penultimate poem, "Terence, This Is Stupid Stuff," justifies Housman's own peculiar treatment of the theme and details, again with allusions to *Paradise Lost,* the manner in which his resolution differs from Milton's more traditional one.

It is, in fact, in the final two poems that Housman achieves the full resolution of his theme, but Lyric LXII is much more relevant to the poet's defense of the poetry of *A Shropshire Lad,* for it is directly concerned with the theme and tone of all the preceding poems. The persona, who has been variously the soldier, the young rustic, the lover, the exile, now becomes the poet, and the poem is the poet's apologia.[3] Through the use of further allusions to Milton and his poetic tradition, Housman manages not only to defend his poetic practice but also to place his work in the larger context of the English poetic tradition.

The first fourteen lines of Lyric LXII voice the objection that the poet rightly anticipated his work would encounter—the charge that it is too despondent:

"Terence, this is stupid stuff:

[2] See William Empson, *Some Versions of Pastoral* (Norfolk, Conn., 1960), pp. 141–83. Empson points out that Milton's treatment of the Eden myth in *Paradise Lost* is quite close to the pastoral tradition.

[3] Of course, in the convention of the work, Terence is the author of all the poems. Housman, it may be recalled, had originally intended to entitle the work *Poems by Terence Hearsay,* but was persuaded to change the title to *A Shropshire Lad* on the suggestion of his friend A. W. Pollard. See Richards, p. 71.

> You eat your victuals fast enough;
> There can't be much amiss, 'tis clear,
> To see the rate you drink your beer.
> But oh, good Lord, the verse you make,
> It gives a chap the belly-ache.
> The cow, the old cow, she is dead;
> It sleeps well, the horned head:
> We poor lads, 'tis our turn now
> To hear such tunes as killed the cow.
> Pretty friendship 'tis to rhyme
> Your friends to death before their time
> Moping melancholy mad:
> Come, pipe a tune to dance to, lad."
>
> (ll. 1–14)

The lighthearted tone of the poem should not obscure its importance. In fact, one of the ironies of the poem is that while the poet is accused of being too serious, his justification for his seriousness is given in the form of light verse. Thus one might expect that some significance lies behind the mockery of the poem. It is also clear that Terence's friend, who makes the charge that his poems are too despondent, is depicted ironically, for he fails to comprehend the significance of his own words. The allusion to the "horned head" of the dead cow suggests obliquely the mythological gates of horn, through which true dreams come. Thus the old cow "sleeps well" after hearing Terence's tunes, but the friend, like Eliot's Sweeney, "guards the horned gates,"[4] i.e., refuses to accept the truth of Terence's poetry. Furthermore, the friend naïvely asserts the source of Terence's poetry in a veiled allusion to *Paradise Lost*. Line 13, "Moping melancholy mad," is an echo of lines 485–86 of Book XI of *Paradise Lost*: "moping melancholy / And moon-struck madness. . . ."[5] The lines appear in a passage in which Adam is first shown the results of his fall from innocence:

[4] "Sweeney Among the Nightingales," 1. 8, from T. S. Eliot, *The Waste Land and Other Poems* (New York, 1962).

[5] This allusion was first pointed out by George O. Marshall, "A Miltonic Echo in Housman," *Notes and Queries*, New Series, V (1958), 258.

> Immediately a place
> Before his eyes appeared, sad, noisome, dark,
> A lazar-house it seemed, wherein were laid
> Numbers of all diseased, all maladies
> Of ghostly spasm, or racking torture, qualms
> Of heart-sick agony, all feverous kinds,
> Convulsions, epilepsies, fierce catarrh,
> Intestine stone and ulcer, colic pangs,
> Demoniac frenzy, moping melancholy
> And moon-struck madness, pining atrophy,
> Marasmus, and wide-wasting pestilence,
> Dropsies and asthmas, and joint-racking rheums.
>
> (XI, 477–88)

George Marshall points out that Housman's poem "adds one more potential cause of death to Milton's list of fatal maladies—the possibility of being rhymed to death by one's friend's despondent poetry."[6] But the context in which Milton's lines appear in *Paradise Lost,* coupled with the second allusion to Milton in Terence's answer to his friend's complaint in lines 21–22, suggests an even more significant parallel between the two works. Adam's anguish over the discovery of the misery and death which result from the loss of innocence is exactly that which the poet depicts in the poems to which his friend objects. In fact, Adam's reaction to viewing the scene to which Housman alludes is quite similar to that of the persona to the recognition of death and decay in a great number of the poems of *A Shropshire Lad.* Adam questions the value of life in the face of certain death:

> "Why is life given
> To be thus wrested from us? rather why
> Obtruded on us thus? who if we knew
> What we receive, would either not accept
> Life offered, or soon beg to lay it down,
> Glad to be so dismissed in peace."
>
> (XI, 502–507)

6 *Ibid.*

The Frame Poems

This is almost exactly the attitude of the persona in the last stanza of Lyric XLVIII of *A Shropshire Lad*:

> Ay, look: high heaven and earth ail from the prime foundation;
>   All thoughts to rive the heart are here, and all are vain:
> Horror and scorn and hate and fear and indignation—
>   Oh why did I awake? when shall I sleep again?
>
> (ll. 13–16)

Terence, like Milton, is concerned with the transition from a perception of life characterized by innocence (Adam's innocence in Eden and the Shropshire lad's early innocence in Shropshire) to one characterized by the discovery that the essential facts of existence are mutability and death.

Terence's answer to his friend's charge in Lyric LXII is a more obvious reference to Milton's purpose in *Paradise Lost*.

> Why, if 'tis dancing you would be,
> There's brisker pipes than poetry.
> Say, for what were hop-yards meant,
> Or why was Burton built on Trent?
> Oh many a peer of England brews
> Livelier liquor than the Muse,
> And malt does more than Milton can
> To justify God's ways to man.
>
> (ll. 15–22)

While the objection to the poet's verses alludes to the loss of innocence and consequent recognition of human evil and death, the poet's reply says something about Milton's attempt to justify the human condition and his own attempt. Milton's efforts to "justify God's ways to man" are not entirely successful, since "malt does more than Milton can." Yet malt, real malt, is not the answer either, since it leads one "to see the world as the world's not" (l. 26). Terence recalls his own experience with Ludlow beer:

> ... down in lovely muck I've lain,
> Happy till I woke again.
> Then I saw the morning sky:

85

> Heigho, the tale was all a lie;
> The world, it was the old world yet,
> I was I, my things were wet,
> And nothing now remained to do
> But begin the game anew.
>
> (ll. 35–42)

But the poet describes his own poetry as a kind of malt:

> 'Tis true, the stuff I bring for sale
> Is not so brisk a brew as ale:
> Out of a stem that scored the hand
> I wrung it in a weary land.
>
> (ll. 49–52)

The image of lines 51 and 52, that of a hand squeezing the juice from a plant, implies a comparison between writing poetry and distilling strong drink. Yet the source for Terence's brew is "a weary land," and the stem from which the juice flows is thorny (it "scored the hand"). His draught is therefore bitter, but therein lies its virtue: ". . . if the smack is sour, / The better for the embittered hour" (ll. 53–54).

Terence next provides an illustration of the value of his own malt as contrasted to the example (ll. 29–42) which revealed the futility of ordinary drink. It is the parable of Mithridates, who withstood death by taking poison in small doses until he acquired immunity:

> He gathered all that springs to birth
> From the many-venomed earth;
> First a little, thence to more,
> He sampled all her killing store;
> And easy, smiling, seasoned sound,
> Sate the king when healths went round. . . .
> —I tell the tale that I heard told.
> Mithridates, he died old.
>
> (ll. 63–68, 75–76)

The poisonous brew of Mithridates is, of course, emblematic

of Terence's own verse, and in the parable of the king who sampled from the "many-venomed earth" all "her killing store," then "died old," he exemplifies the value of his poetry.

To read "Terence . . ." as a statement of Housman's defense of the kind of poetry found in *A Shropshire Lad*—that is, to assume that just as Terence shares Housman's "view of life" he shares his view of art[7]—is to conclude that the poet feels his own work and Milton's *Paradise Lost* share a common concern, however much they differ in style and form. The allusions to *Paradise Lost* point to the fact that both works spring from an attempt to deal with the human condition as characterized by mutability and death. Housman writes in his own way of

> . . . the fruit
> Of that forbidden tree, whose mortal taste
> Brought death into the world and all our woe. . . .

But in *A Shropshire Lad* the Tree of the Knowledge of Good and Evil is the cherry, by which the innocent first perceives that his days are limited to "three score years and ten," and Eden after the Fall becomes the pastoral Shropshire, from which Terence is ultimately exiled. Milton's mythopoeic justification of the ills of human existence is replaced in *A Shropshire Lad* by a view which sees the universe, not in terms of myth, but in terms of what Cleanth Brooks has called "the scientific neutralization of nature."[8] That is, the supernatural framework is removed and Housman is forced to justify human ills in naturalistic terms. John Stevenson has made a similar point in a comparison of Housman and Wordsworth:

> . . . whereas Wordsworth could accept earnestly and devoutly the doctrine of nature's divinity, Housman could only accept the attitude toward nature that looks toward

[7] See Housman's letter to Pollet quoted in Norman Marlow, *A. E. Housman: Scholar and Poet*, p. 150. Housman says, in part, "The Shropshire Lad is an imaginary figure, with something of my temperament and view of life."

[8] Quoted by John Stevenson, "Housman's Lyric Tradition," *Forum*, IV (1962), 19.

the modern world. . . . The early sympathy is gone, and alienation has set in to complicate the vision. It is just here that the modern attitude is found because with the strong awareness of incongruity, of the ambiguity between belief and fact, there begins the redefining and the reappraisal which marks the beginnings of modern literature.[9]

Thus the imagery by which the poetry of *A Shropshire Lad* is characterized in Housman's apologia is particularly appropriate. It is first a bitter brew which has been wrung from a thorny plant growing in "a weary land." Secondly, it is compared to a poisonous drink which is gathered from the "many-venomed earth." The imagery suggests a poetry which has its source in exactly those kinds of human experience which earlier poets had tried to transcend through the use of myth or a spiritualization of nature. Yet Terence's point in Lyric LXII is that only through an honest appraisal of his situation does man progress, like the Shropshire lad himself throughout the course of the sixty-three lyrics of the work, from the naïveté of youth to the resignation of manhood. Therefore, the poetry is as a bitter malt brewed from the ills of life by which man may come to understand and accept his own condition. It is this malt, Terence subtly implies, which "does more than Milton can / To justify God's ways to man."

The final lyric of *A Shropshire Lad* continues the metaphor of the poetry as a product of the earth itself, but here the image shifts slightly with new suggestions and allusions. The poems are now plants which spring from the soil through the care and attention of the poet:

> I hoed and trenched and weeded,
> And took the flowers to fair:
> I brought them home unheeded;
> The hue was not the wear.
>
> (ll. 1–4)

9 *Ibid.*

The poem continues the metaphor with further implications; the flowers bear seeds, which will be sown about the land:

> So up and down I sow them
> For lads like me to find,
> When I shall lie below them,
> A dead man out of mind.
>
> Some seed the birds devour,
> And some the season mars,
> But here and there will flower
> The solitary stars. . . .
>
> (ll. 5–12)

The allusion here is to Christ's parable of the sower of seeds,[10] for the poem is the poet's parable of the value of his poetry. And contrary to the weight of opinion which presents Housman's poetry as an essentially negative force, Lyric LXIII proposes a positive worth for the poems. In the last poem of the volume as in the first, Housman is concerned with the paradox of permanence and change. The individual must perish; generic man survives, and the final two lyrics of *A Shropshire Lad* reveal the poet's sense of his responsibility to man. His work traces one pattern of universal human experience—the growth from innocence to experience, from a sense of stability to the consciousness of decay. The poems, individually, work out some of the implications of this experience; collectively, they give it form. The final lyrics, however, add another dimension to the mutability-permanence pattern. In Lyrics LXII and LXIII the poetry itself provides the poet a means to transcend his own mutable nature. Poetry as a product of the mind of man has a permanence which is denied man himself. Housman recognized this when he said in effect (at his inaugural address at University College, London) that the products of the mind are the least perishable of pleasures, "the least subject to . . . the wear

---

10 This parable is found in the Gospel of St. Mark, IV: 3–8.

of time."[11] In "Terence . . . ," poetry enables man to overcome
the limitations of his mutable nature, to bridge the gap of gen-
erations. Terence says of his poetry:

> It should do good to heart and head
> When your soul is in my soul's stead;
> And I will friend you, if I may,
> In the dark and cloudy day.
>
> (ll. 55–58)

In the imagery of the final poem, Housman's poetry achieves
the permanence of physical nature, which in the succession of
the seasons experiences a rebirth which the naturalistic doctrine denies man. In the last stanza of *A Shropshire Lad,* the
poet says concerning the "flowers," or poems, of the volume:

> And fields will yearly bear them
> As light-leaved spring comes on,
> And luckless lads will wear them
> When I am dead and gone.
>
> (ll. 13-16)

Christ explained that his parable of the sower should be interpreted as an account of the reception of his words among
the people who followed him. Housman's parable may be simi-
larly interpreted. The last stanza of Lyric LXIII is a statement
of the final triumph of art over the forces of change. There is
a sense of resolution, of finality, in the poem. The poet's quest
for permanence has been achieved, in one sense, although his
resolution is in itself paradoxical. He has overcome time
through a metaphorical conception of the immortality of art,
but the subject of that art is the ultimate victory of time over
man. On a more practical level, the most that can be hoped for
is that the poet's insights into the human problems that he
considers will remain "for lads like me to find," when the poet
himself, time's victim, lies "a dead man out of mind."

Clearly, then, the ordering of the three poems which intro-

---

11 See *A. E. Housman: Selected Prose,* ed. by John Carter, p. 20.

duce and conclude *A Shropshire Lad* can be justified. But, more important, the scaffolding which these poems constitute contributes greatly to any interpretation of the work as a whole. The reader has been provided, particularly through the Miltonic allusions, a context or tradition within which to consider the sixty remaining lyrics. If he ignores that context and Housman's use of the tradition, as well as his departure from it, he risks not only a capricious reading of *A Shropshire Lad* but also a misunderstanding of the nature of Housman's art.

VI

THE SHROPSHIRE POEMS

*T*he common conception of *A Shropshire Lad* as a collection in which the poems are gathered indiscriminately has had the unfortunate consequence of encouraging the reader to ignore the distinct movement of theme and tone signaled by the shift in setting. The title has prompted the misconception that the work is set entirely in Shropshire; but this is hardly the case, any more than there is any truth in the belief of some of Housman's early readers that he was a Shropshire poet. This belief was more easily corrected by the facts, as Housman reported them in a letter to Maurice Pollet:

> I was born in Worcestershire, not Shropshire, where I have never spent much time. . . . I had a sentimental feeling for Shropshire because its hills were our western horizon. I know Ludlow and Wenlock, but my topographical details—Hughley, Abdon under Clee,—are sometimes quite wrong.[1]

The errors in topographical reference were not especially important to Housman because, as he explained elsewhere, ". . . my Shropshire, like the Cambridge of Lycidas, is not exactly a real place. . . ."[2] The fact that Housman's Shropshire is not real but symbolic makes even more imperative an examination

---

[1] Maurice Pollet, "Lettre inédite de A. E. Housman," *Etudes Anglaises,* V (1937), 403.

[2] Cyril Clemens, "Some Unpublished Housman Letters," *Poet Lore,* LIII (1947), 262. The belief that Housman spent his boyhood in Shropshire has, however, persisted, as evidenced by this statement in an es-

of his use of the Shropshire setting, especially as change of location corresponds to a shift in the point of view of the persona of his lyrics.

That all of Housman's poems do not depend upon the reality of the Shropshire setting has been demonstrated by the recent study of Ralph Franklin, who showed that only fifteen of the sixty-three poems contain references to Shropshire, a number of these recognized by the poet as inaccurate.[3] Yet Franklin's study does not distinguish between the poems which derive their tone from the Shropshire setting and those which are set outside Shropshire and marked by the nostalgic recollection of names and places which have become alien to the persona. This distinction is of primary importance in the design of the work as a whole.

An examination of the poems which preserves the integrity of their order reveals that only the first thirty-six are set in Shropshire; the remainder, principally in London. Moreover, changes made in the printer's copy of *A Shropshire Lad* immediately before its publication tend to emphasize the shift in setting, almost as if Housman were taking special pains to highlight a transition which might otherwise escape notice. Tom Burns Haber's listing of the last-minute alterations made in the printer's copy (now in the library of Trinity College, Cambridge) shows that Housman deleted five poems, three of which later appeared in *Last Poems,* shifted the ordering of a large number of the other lyrics, and added three, which appear in the final arrangement as Nos. XXXIV, XXXVII, and XLI.[4] The three insertions and much of the reordering clearly strengthen the sense of relocation in setting. The deletions may have been made because the poems obscured the pattern upon

---

say published in 1967: "His poetry was distinctly a product of his youth, and even then of a retrospective youth—the Shropshire adolescence recollected in the London of the Nineties (Housman's Twenties) ."— Brooks Otis, "Housman and Horace," *Pacific Coast Philology*, II (1967), 5.

3 "Housman's Shropshire," *MLQ*, XXIV (1963), 164–71.

4 See "The Printer's Copy of *A Shropshire Lad*" in *The Manuscript*

which the poet wished to focus attention. Although such a conjecture can never be definitely established, it is supported by the fact that Housman considered three of the deleted poems of sufficient worth to be published later.

Perhaps the most significant addition was Lyric XXXVII, which recounts the journey of the persona from Shropshire to London. Housman's use of more obvious narrative techniques in this poem, particularly his use of the couplet rather than his customary ballad stanza (or some variation of it), sets it apart from the less specific lyrical mode of the verses surrounding it. It opens with the familiar landscape of Shropshire vanishing from sight in the west as the train carries Terence to London:

> As through the wild green hills of Wyre
> The train ran, changing sky and shire,
> And far behind, a fading crest,
> Low in the forsaken west
> Sank the high-reared head of Clee,
> My hand lay empty on my knee.
> Aching on my knee it lay:
> That morning half a shire away
> So many an honest fellow's fist
> Had well nigh wrung it from the wrist.
>
> (ll. 1–10)

The poet's concentration on the narrative element suggests that Lyric XXXVII was inserted as a functional poem to mark the break between the preceding group of Shropshire poems and the exile poems which follow. It looks backward to the Shropshire setting and ahead to the London exile. The poem alludes to the pastoral setting in these lines:

> And if my foot returns no more
> To Teme nor Corve nor Severn shore,

Poems of A. E. Housman (Minneapolis, 1955), pp. 120–29. The poems which were deleted but later published by Housman in *Last Poems* are, "In the Morning, in the Morning," which became No. XXIII; "Yonder See the Morning Blink," which became No. XI; and "Her Strong Enchantments Failing," which became No. III.

> Luck, my lads, be with you still
> By falling stream and standing hill,
> By chiming tower and whispering tree,
> Men that made a man of me.
> About your work in town and farm
> Still you'll keep my head from harm,
> Still you'll help me, hands that gave
> A grasp to friend me to the grave.
>
> (ll. 27–36)

The "falling stream and standing hill" recall the scene on Wenlock Edge in Lyric XXXI, as well as the first two lines of Lyric XXXV; the "chiming tower" is obviously Ludlow Tower, which plays "The Conquering Hero Comes" in "The Recruit";[5] and the "whispering tree" may be an allusion to the cherry in Lyric II, which reminded the young innocent of his "threescore years and ten," or the aspen of Lyric XXVI, whose whispering leaves told of the inconstancy of love. But the loneliness and anxiety of the London poems are also anticipated. In one passage, Terence addresses the hand which still aches from the handshakes at his departure:

> You and I must keep from shame
> In London streets the Shropshire name;
> On banks of Thames they must not say
> Severn breeds worse men than they;
> And friends abroad must bear in mind
> Friends at home they leave behind.
> Oh, I shall be stiff and cold
> When I forget you, hearts of gold;
> The land where I shall mind you not
> Is the land where all's forgot.
>
> (ll. 17–26)

5 Ralph Franklin has pointed out that the reference in "The Recruit" to the tower which chimes "The Conquering Hero Comes" is quite accurate. Housman was referring to the tower of the Church of St. Lawrence, known locally as Ludlow tower, which chimes "See, the conqu'ring hero comes," a chorus from Part III of Handel's *Judas Maccabaeus*. See "Housman's Shropshire," pp. 164–71, for a full account of the accuracy of his use of Shropshire place names.

The argument that this poem was added to make the shift in setting more pronounced is supported also by the fact that other changes Housman made at the same time strengthen the sense of relocation immediately after it. He also added Lyric XLI, beginning "In my own shire, if I was sad, . . ." which helps to contrast the pastoral existence of the old shire with life in London, as does Lyric XXXIX, which is constructed on the theme of the persona's imaginative contrast of spring in London and in "Wenlock town." Lyric XXXIX was moved from its original position as No. XLIII.[6]

Housman's third and final addition to the printer's copy of *A Shropshire Lad* may also be related to the journey from Shropshire. The poem, entitled "The New Mistress," became Lyric XXXIV, replacing "Yonder See the Morning Blink." A comparison of the two poems shows that "The New Mistress" was an apt replacement, not so much because of its superior poetic merit (the poem it replaced was later published as No. XI of *Last Poems*), but because it fit more neatly into the motif Housman had established in Lyrics XXXII-XXXVIII. The addition of "The New Mistress" reinforces the journey metaphor contained in the five poems preceding Lyric XXXVII since it is concerned with a lad who leaves his home shire and his old mistress to become a soldier of the Queen.

The journey is prompted by the misfortunes of love. It opens with the parting words of the old mistress:

> "Oh, sick I am to see you, will you never let me be?
> You may be good for something but you are not good for me.
> Oh, go where you are wanted, for you are not wanted here.
> And that was all the farewell when I parted from my dear."
>
> (ll. 1–4)

The title offers a key to the poem's imagery and theme. By repeating certain phrases of the first stanza which characterized

---

[6] These poems will be discussed in more detail in the following chapter, devoted to the exile poems.

the old mistress, the persona indicates the identity of the new one. In stanza 2 she is the Queen:

"I will go where I am wanted, to a lady born and bred
Who will dress me free for nothing in a uniform of red;
She will not be sick to see me if I only keep it clean:
I will go where I am wanted for a soldier of the Queen."

(ll. 5–8)

By continuing the same pattern of repetition in the last two stanzas the poet suggests the ambiguity of the title. It refers also to the lad's sergeant:

"I will go where I am wanted, for the sergeant does not mind;
He may be sick to see me but he treats me very kind:
He gives me beer and breakfast and a ribbon for my cap,
And I never knew a sweetheart spend her money on a chap."

(ll. 9–12)

Finally, in the last stanza the title is extended to include the " 'enemies of England,' " with the suggestion that the soldier's final mistress may be death:

"I will go where I am wanted, where there's room for one or two,
And the men are none too many for the work there is to do;
Where the standing line wears thinner and the dropping dead
    lie thick;
And the enemies of England they shall see me and be sick."

(ll. 13–16)

The effectiveness of Housman's use of the controlling love imagery to characterize war may be seen in the ambiguities of the last stanza. The soldier, metaphorically the suitor in the courtship of war, is finally where he is wanted, for the new mistress, unlike the old, has " 'room for one or two.' " The soldier may also achieve the consummation of the courtship with his new mistress, for " 'the standing line wears thinner.' " This phrase may be taken literally as the battle line; but metaphorically, to continue the image pattern of the poem, it may be taken as the line of suitors who wait to achieve the logical end of their roles as soldier-lovers, death (" 'the dropping dead lie thick' ") . Housman's imagery here thus achieves perfect consistency on both the literal and the metaphorical level (dying, of course, is traditionally a metaphor for the consummation of the sex act) . The poem is interesting in itself, but its use of the motif of the journey of death is an even more significant consideration in seeking an answer to the question of why the poet inserted it in its present position, for the two preceding poems and the two which follow also use the metaphor of the journey as a basic structuring device.

The following lyric (No. XXXV) makes even more explicit that the soldier's journey is to certain death. It opens with a distant call to battle, which the country lad hears in the comfort of the "idle hill of summer, / Sleepy with the flow of streams" (ll. 1–2) . Seeing others make the journey, he knows their fate:

> Far and near and low and louder
> On the roads of earth go by,
> Dear to friends and food for powder,
> Soldiers marching, all to die.
>
> (ll. 5–8)

But in spite of the realization that the march leads to certain death the youth asserts that he has no choice except to join it: "Woman bore me, I will rise" (l. 16) . The following poem (No. XXXVI) returns to the theme of the lover who journeys from his love: "White in the moon the long road lies / That leads me from my love" (ll. 3–4) . The lover's only consolation is the conceit that since the earth is round, the road he takes away from his home will eventually lead him back.[7]

The two poems which precede "The New Mistress" (XXXII and XXXIII) are concerned primarily with death, but they depict death as a journey. In Lyric XXXII life is a momentary resting place in an endless trek. The transitory state of life is like the passing of the winds, which blew "from far" the "stuff

---

[7] See Ch. II for a more detailed discussion of these two poems in terms of Housman's use of the personae of the soldier and the lover.

of life to knit me." Man tarries "for a breath," then takes his "endless way." This conception of death is continued in Lyric XXXIII, which begins by speaking of death in literal terms ("I think the love I bear you / Should make you not to die" [ll. 3–4]) but ends with the image of death as a journey to a distant town:

> But now, since all is idle,
>   To this lost heart be kind,
> Ere to a town you journey
>   Where friends are ill to find.
>   (ll. 13–16)

An analysis of this group of five poems thus accounts, at least in part, for the addition of Lyric XXXVII and "The New Mistress," as well as the deletion of "Yonder See the Morning Blink." "The New Mistress" conforms to the pattern established in the poems surrounding it, unlike the poem it replaced. But the movement away from the home shire is only obliquely present in Lyrics XXXII–XXXVI. The insertion of Lyric XXXVII focuses attention on the departure from Shropshire as the preceding five poems had not done by picking up the thread of the narrative and depicting the Shropshire lad himself leaving the land of his youth. It is clear that the persona of Lyric XXXVII is, in fact, Terence because Housman was careful to distinguish the poems in which Terence is the speaker from those, like "The New Mistress," narrated by others. He does this by enclosing the latter in quotation marks. Only four poems appear as complete quotations in *A Shropshire Lad*— "The New Mistress," Lyric VIII ("Farewell to Barn and Stack and Tree"), "The Carpenter's Son," and "The Day of Battle." The situation described in each of these poems precludes the Shropshire lad himself from being the speaker, and Housman preserves the integrity of his arrangement by so indicating with his punctuation.[8]

---

8 Haber's refusal to consider the collection a unified work causes him to miss the mark with his own explanation of Housman's punctua-

The six transition poems are important in clarifying the symbolic value of the Shropshire setting. When Housman, in describing his Shropshire as "not exactly a real place," compared it to the Cambridge of *Lycidas,* he provided a key to an understanding of its true function, for the symbolic associations involved in the transfer from Shropshire to London should be regarded as a part of the pastoral tradition to which both *A Shropshire Lad* and *Lycidas* belong. Shropshire is, in effect, the pastoral Arcadia. Like Milton's Cambridge in *Lycidas,* it does not conform to the real land whose place names and geography it adopts, but instead provides the environment for the experience which the poet is able to recount only through the pastoral mask. William Empson has observed that the pastoral process works by putting the complex into the simple.[9] One observes this process in the opening poems of *A Shropshire Lad.* The complexities of life have been reduced to a level which can be communicated, and this simplicity is made possible through the convention that the poet is a rustic youth named Terence whose initial lack of sophistication and closeness to the primal forces of life allow him to comment meaningfully on the human situation. Housman, the sophisticated scholar, thus avoids the sentimentality which is always dangerously near in dealing with the commonplaces of human experience. Terence, however, is able to express the simple and obvious truths of his own insight since he is unaware that these feelings have been expressed before in much more sophisticated ways.[10]

---

tion. He asks of "The Day of Battle": "Why were the signs of quotation added? Probably as a movement of retreat from the immediacy of the grim statement of the lyric. . . . A similar motive may have been behind the use of quotation marks about the heretical lyric number 47, 'The Carpenter's Son'" (*The Manuscript Poems of A. E. Housman,* p. 124). He ignores the more obvious answer that the quotation marks indicate poems narrated by someone other than Terence.

[9] *Some Versions of Pastoral,* p. 23.

[10] For a discussion of the implications of Housman's pastoral mask see John Stevenson, "The Pastoral Setting in the Poetry of A. E. Housman,"

Although Housman's debt to the pastoral tradition is important, especially as it enables him to treat one of the most persistent themes of literature without becoming maudlin or betraying his own voice, his departure from the tradition is even more crucial to the structure of *A Shropshire Lad*. For Housman's pastoral persona is not a static character; in fact, the dominant pattern in the Shropshire poems is the growth of awareness and sophistication in the persona which eventually brings about his departure from the pastoral land. *A Shropshire Lad* begins by putting the complex into the simple, and the poet maintains the pastoral mask throughout the sixty-three poems of the volume; but as the work unfolds, the simplicity of the persona and his earlier sympathetic unity with the pastoral scene are threatened and finally destroyed as his vision is expanded.

This pattern may be traced through the Shropshire poems, but it must be borne in mind that the development which eventually leads to the departure from the symbolic land of innocence is not one which can always be followed poem by poem. Housman's method of composition precluded this kind of consistent progression, since the poems were not composed in the order in which they were finally arranged. Instead, the movement is marked by stages, by series of poems which signal new directions in the persona's awareness and a gradual disintegration of his initial harmony with the world around him which ends finally in complete alienation.

South Atlantic Quarterly, LV (1956), 487–500. I am indebted to Stevenson's perceptive analysis of Housman's pastoral mode; however, he seems to regard Housman's persona as an essentially static character. He makes no distinction between the persona of the early poems of *A Shropshire Lad* and those which follow his departure from the pastoral scene. See also R. L. Kowalczyk, "Horatian Tradition and Pastoral Mode in Housman's *A Shropshire Lad*," *Victorian Poetry*, IV (1966), 223–35. Kowalczyk, too, treats Housman's Terence as a static pastoral figure. He states that "although one cannot argue that *A Shropshire Lad* contains an architectonic structure, the pastoral mode produces a unifying and controlling effect upon the cycle of Lyrics" (p. 235).

The innocent's view of himself as a part of the external world is first threatened in the opening poem within the frame, "Loveliest of Trees." Here he discovers his own mortality in calculating his Biblical threescore years and ten; but at this point his consciousness of death is no more than an abstraction, and at the conclusion of the poem he still retains some sympathy with nature ("About the woodland I will go / To see the cherry hung with snow"). This harmony is weakened by his awareness that while nature is perpetually reborn he has but "fifty springs" to enjoy its beauty; yet the tone is not, as it later becomes in the work, one of complete disillusionment. It is true that the following lyric, "The Recruit," is marked by an ironic undertone which qualifies its optimism with the hint that even the symbol of permanence in the poem, Ludlow tower, is destined for eventual destruction; but No. IV, "Reveille," as its title implies, is a call for involvement in an existence which has positive value in spite of its brevity:

> Towns and countries woo together,
>   Forelands beacon, belfries call;
> Never lad that trod on leather
>   Lived to feast his heart with all.
>
> Up, lad: thews that lie and cumber
>   Sunlit pallets never thrive;
> Morns abed and daylight slumber
>   Were not meant for man alive.
>
> (ll. 13–20)

The optimism of youth is still strong when, in Lyric VII, the country lad strides "blithe afield" only to be reminded by the song of a bird that his optimism is mistaken:

> "Lie down, lie down, young yeoman;
>   What use to rise and rise?
> Rise man a thousand mornings
>   Yet down at last he lies,
>   And then the man is wise."
>
> (ll. 11–15)

The youth rebels against this fatalism and attempts to still the voice of doubt for which the blackbird is emblematic:

> I picked a stone and aimed it
> And threw it with a will:
> Then the bird was still.
> (ll. 18–20)

But the bird's song has become a permanent part of the speaker's own awareness: "Then my soul within me / Took up the blackbird's strain" (ll. 21–22). Henceforth he is preoccupied with death and decay, and what was before only an intellectual awareness is made concrete in the two poems which follow; for here, for the first time, death becomes a reality. In Lyric VIII, Terence discovers that his friend is a murderer and sees that the sin of Cain forces the murderer's departure from "Severn shore." In Lyric IX he awaits the murderer's execution:

> They hang us now in Shrewsbury jail:
> The whistles blow forlorn,
> And trains all night groan on the rail
> To men that die at morn.
> (ll. 9–12)

The pastoral Eden has been blighted by the unmentionable odor of death, and the sense of disillusionment and alienation is now pervasive. The poems which follow reveal the extent to which the death-thoughts color the youth's perception of his world.

As he watches the pageant of life parade before him in Lyric XII, he is reminded that his "house of flesh" will soon be replaced by the "house of dust." But for the first time he views death in a new light, for he sees it as a source for the kind of permanence which the flesh denies him. Death is now a preservative, at least in the conceit of the youth who seeks to regain his lost innocence; and lovers who die as bride and bridegroom are forever so:

> Lovers lying two and two
> Ask not whom they sleep beside,

> And the bridegroom all night through
> Never turns him to the bride.
>
> (ll. 13–16)

This preoccupation with death as the agent which halts human transience is continued in "To an Athlete Dying Young," where death is imaged as a victory in a race which all men must run. In the following poem, No. XX, the speaker pursues his new conception of death to its logical conclusion by contemplating suicide:

> These are the thoughts I often think
> As I stand gazing down
> In act upon the cressy brink
> To strip and dive and drown....
>
> (ll. 9–12)

Three poems later, at Ludlow fair in Lyric XXIII, he is again reminded that through death man may flee "the fields where glory does not stay." He notes that among the "lads in their hundreds" who come in for the fair is a small group of men who will "carry back bright to the coiner the mintage of man." These are "the lads who will die in their glory and never be old" (ll. 15–16). In this series of poems the lad thus seeks an escape from the inevitability of his transient existence. His solution, no more than an intellectual conceit, fails as a practical measure; but it serves to ease the anguish which is itself the product of a mental process, a way of looking at the world.

The persona finds some comfort also in the recognition that his loss of a simple and innocent harmony with nature is not a singular experience. In the final two Shropshire poems (XXX and XXXI) his view is extended beyond himself:

> Others, I am not the first,
> Have willed more mischief than they durst:
> If in the breathless night I too
> Shiver now, 'tis nothing new.
>
> (XXX, ll. 1–4)

The scene of Lyric XXXI is itself symbolic of the persona's larger perspective of the plight he shares with all mankind. The English yeoman who watches the "old wind in the old anger" wreak its destruction on the wood imagines the scene as it must have appeared centuries before:

> Then, 'twas before my time, the Roman
> At yonder heaving hill would stare:
> The blood that warms an English yeoman,
> The thoughts that hurt him, they were there.
>
> There, like the wind through woods in riot,
> Through him the gale of life blew high;
> The tree of man was never quiet:
> Then 'twas the Roman, now 'tis I.
>
> (ll. 9–16)

Housman's rustic has thus achieved a measure of sophistication. His once personal and provincial outlook has been broadened; his discovery of a mutable and painful world of death, initially within himself, is no longer contained within, and his departure from the pastoral land of Shropshire is thus anticipated.

Intermingled with the poems summarized above and paralleling the development of the rustic's discovery of the world of change and death are the love lyrics, which depict a progressive awareness that love, like life, is fleeting and transient. The earliest love poem, No. V, is lighthearted in tone in spite of its theme of love's misfortunes. Lyric X describes a world at its prime in which the young man experiences the forces of life quickening around him. He sees that "In farm and field through all the shire / The eye beholds the heart's desire" (ll. 17–18), and is therefore strengthened in his belief that the pattern of life dictates that his present lovesickness may soon be cured: "For lovers should be loved again" (l. 20). It is Lyric XIII, "One-and-Twenty," which marks the turning point in the youth's attitude toward love, as his sudden maturity reveals to him the true nature of human affections. At twenty-one he was

warned by a "wise man" that love would bring " 'endless rue' ";
"And I am two-and-twenty, / And oh, 'tis true, 'tis true" (ll. 15–
16). Hereafter the lighthearted view of love is replaced by a
more painful one.

Housman's notation in the printer's copy of *A Shropshire
Lad* indicates that he conceived of Lyric XIII as the introduction to a whole group of poems which depict the true transiency
of love. At the top of the page on which the poem appears,
Housman wrote "Another Series."[11] The five poems that follow deal in more detail with the various stages of the misery of
the lad who fails to heed the wise man's advice and gives his
heart away. In No. XIV the lover's despair is such that seemingly it can never be removed:

> There flowers no balm to sain him
> From east of earth to west
> That's lost for everlasting
> The heart out of his breast.
>
> Here by the labouring highway
> With empty hands I stroll:
> Sea-deep, till doomsday morning,
> Lie lost my heart and soul.
>   (ll. 13–20)

Yet in the last poem of the series, No. XVIII, he is quite himself again. His own quick recovery is ironic in reinforcing
the transience of all human emotions, even those which appear
to be the most enduring:

> Oh, when I was in love with you,
> Then I was clean and brave,
> And miles around the wonder grew
> How well did I behave.
>
> And now the fancy passes by,
> And nothing will remain,
> And miles around they'll say that I
> Am quite myself again.

11 See Haber, *The Manuscript Poems of A. E. Housman*, p. 123.

A progressively tragic view of love is shown in the later Shropshire poems. The theme of "Bredon Hill" (No. XXI) is the impossibility of lasting love in a world blighted by death; and the final series of love poems in the Shropshire group (Nos. XXV, XXVI, and XXVII) deals with the true pathos of love, for all three poems reveal that the memory of love is short. A lover who dies is quickly forgotten, his place taken by his rival. This increasingly darkened view of love parallels the loss of the persona's simple acceptance of the natural world and his unity with it. As he is estranged from his land and the forces in operation within it, his estrangement is evidenced by the loss of the earlier child's view of human affection as something enduring. By the end of the Shropshire cycle the estrangement is complete; the next step is the departure from Shropshire. The fallen innocent must be banished from his Eden.

This summary of the Shropshire poems has omitted discussion of only those few poems which do not materially affect the pattern recorded above. The ordering of the Shropshire group is, in fact, loose enough so that the position of some individual poems could be shifted without obscuring the overall design. Housman obviously arranged the sequence of poems after their composition, with possibly one or two exceptions; and his problem was to give order to material which contained only the potential for order as it stood. The importance of discerning the pattern of his design is apparent when one realizes that, to understand completely the lyrics which follow No. XXXVII ("As Through the Wild Green Hills of Wyre") , one must be aware that the scene has changed, as has the tone of the poetry. The poems now look back westward from London to Shropshire, and the mood of the speaker in the poems is now largely one of nostalgia for something lost and never to be recovered.

VII

THE EXILE POEMS

*T*he shift in setting from Shrop-
shire to London, which is effected in Lyric XXXVII, and which
determines with few exceptions the theme and tone of the remainder of the poems of *A Shropshire Lad,* has the immediate
result of reinforcing the persona's sense of loss and his re-
orientation in thought. The theme of estrangement is established in the first four poems of the exile group, three of which
were shifted to their present position in the final ordering,
the fourth ("In My Own Shire, if I Was Sad") added to the
printer's copy immediately before publication.[1] That the collection benefits from the poet's final rearrangement is obvious,
for these four poems, more than any others in *A Shropshire
Lad,* establish the contrast between the pastoral existence of
Shropshire and the exile in London; and the full force of the
stoicism of the later London poems depends, in large measure,
upon the reader's knowledge of the experience of loss from
which it is born.

In the opening poem of the exile group, No. XXXVIII, the
persona's vision is directed back to the west, to the land from
which he has now become estranged:

> The winds out of the west land blow,
>   My friends have breathed them there;
> Warm with the blood of lads I know
>   Comes east the sighing air.

[1] See Tom Burns Haber, "The Printer's Copy of *A Shropshire Lad*" in
The Manuscript Poems of A. E. Housman, pp. 126–27.

> It fanned their temples, filled their lungs,
>   Scattered their forelocks free;
> My friends made words of it with tongues
>   That talk no more to me.
>
>   (ll. 1–8)

Metaphorically, the wind is the life force with which the pastoral youth identified himself in the home shire. This identification is suggested in line 2 ("My friends have breathed them [the winds] there"), and in line 3, which refers to the winds as "warm with the blood of lads I know." In line 4 the wind is the breath of life which "filled their lungs." Housman, in fact, is consistent throughout *A Shropshire Lad* in his use of wind imagery. In Lyric XXXI he refers to the "gale of life" which exists in the observer who watches the wind blow through the woods on Wenlock Edge. The persona of Lyric XXXII states that the "stuff of life" "blew hither" like the wind. The wind of No. XVI may also be identified as the vital force which creates a ceaseless cycle of change, suggested by the nettle tossed about on the grave of the lover "that hanged himself for love."

The correlation between the wind and the intensity of the Shropshire existence is made clear in the last two stanzas of No. XXXVIII, for here it becomes evident that the exile is itself a manifestation of the loss of harmony with the force of life once active in the home shire:

> Oh lads, at home I heard you plain,
>   But here your speech is still,
> And down the sighing wind in vain
>   You hollo from the hill.
>
> The wind and I, we both were there,
>   But neither long abode;
> Now through the friendless world we fare
>   And sigh upon the road.
>
>   (ll. 13–20)

In London, then (or more properly in this poem "upon the road" to London), the alien finds himself in a "friendless world."

The journey from Shropshire makes concrete, both literally and in its symbolic implications, the final break with the world of youth and innocence. The three poems which follow contribute a similar tone, for they, too, look back to a land of youth with nostalgia and perceiving, like Wordsworth's pastoral persona, that ". . . there hath passed away a glory from the earth."[2] Lyrics XXXIX–XLI recall, in the mood of the "Intimations Ode," the hour of "splendor in the grass, of glory in the flower"[3]:

> 'Tis time, I think, by Wenlock town
>   The golden broom should blow;
> The hawthorn sprinkled up and down
>   Should charge the land with snow.
>
> Spring will not wait the loiterer's time
>   Who keeps so long away;
> So others wear the broom and climb
>   The hedgerows heaped with may.
>
> Oh tarnish late on Wenlock Edge,
>   Gold that I never see;
> Lie long, high snowdrifts in the hedge
>   That will not shower on me.
>   (No. XXXIX)

One great difference, however, between Housman's treatment of the loss of harmony with nature in *A Shropshire Lad* and Wordsworth's conception of the same process in a poem like the "Intimations Ode" lies in the fact that Housman depicts the loss not in terms of time but in the motif of two lands, one a land of youth and simplicity, the other a place of exile. In Lyric XL the memories of youth come from "yon far country" of "blue remembered hills." Furthermore, Wordsworth finds compensation, even in the midst of loss, in the memories of youth.[4] To the persona of Lyric XL, however, the remembrance of things past is "an air that kills":

2 "Ode: Intimations of Immortality from Recollections of Early Childhood," l. 17.

3 L. 180.

4 See John Stevenson, "Housman's Lyric Tradition," *Forum,* IV (1962),

> Into my heart an air that kills
> From yon far country blows:
> What are those blue remembered hills,
> What spires, what farms are those?
>
> That is the land of lost content,
> I see it shining plain,
> The happy highways where I went
> And cannot come again.

That the "land of lost content" is Shropshire, as seen through the imagination, should be obvious from the position of the poem in relation to the exile poems surrounding it. However, one recent critic, obviously unaware of the change in setting, finds the reference to the "far country" confusing, although he believes the confusion is deliberate:

> The Shropshire commentator deliberately appears confused here, for Housman submerges the symbolic meaning of "far country." Thus the reader fails to discern whether Terence wishes to describe his Shropshire or the irretrievable past. Terence's confusion suggests that his memory is slowly debilitating and that he finds himself in the present observing a quickly changing world. In both cases, the speaker recognizes that time has robbed him of a sense of permanence and stability, since his fading memory destroys the unchanged past as quickly as his present world changes.[5]

But the speaker does not appear confused when the poem is seen in relation to the design of the whole work. For the home shire is now indeed a "far country," and it is being described not by an inhabitant whose "memory is slowly debilitating," but by an exile who views it only in the imagination ("Into my *heart* an air that kills / From yon far country blows"). Neither is there a real problem on the part of the reader who has followed the development of Housman's persona in dis-

---

17–21, for a comparison of the attitudes toward nature in the poetry of Housman and Wordsworth which I have followed here.

5 R. L. Kowalczyk, "Horatian Tradition and Pastoral Mode in Housman's *A Shropshire Lad*," *Victorian Poetry*, IV (1966), 232.

cerning "whether Terence wishes to describe his Shropshire or the irretrievable past," for they are now one. The land which is seen "shining plain" in the imagination is, much like the past as described in Tennyson's "Tears, Idle Tears," both fresh and strange. It is, as Tennyson pictures it, a kind of "death in life," living in the memory but beyond recovery. Any confusion which arises from a reading of the poem must be laid to the reader's failure to place the poem in its proper context. The critic quoted above, R. L. Kowalczyk, states that ". . . one cannot argue that *A Shropshire Lad* contains an architectonic structure . . . ."[6] Yet it is precisely his lack of attention to the structure of the work that results in a reading which obviously misses the point.

Terence's estrangement from the "land of lost content" should have been clear from the preceding two poems as well as from the poem which follows. No. XLI, "In My Own Shire, if I Was Sad," is constructed on the contrast between the "homely comforters" of the home shire and the "mortal sickness" of London.[7] John Stevenson has called the poem Housman's "Intimations Ode," [8] dealing as it does with the Wordsworthian theme of the therapeutic value of nature. Yet, as Stevenson further observes, Housman's attitude toward nature differs radically from Wordsworth's, primarily because Housman could not accept the Romantic doctrine of nature's divinity. Nature does not teach the persona of "In My Own Shire" intimations of immortality; it serves only as a comforter, sorrowing with youth by displaying "the beautiful and death-struck year":

> In my own shire, if I was sad,
> Homely comforters I had:
> The earth, because my heart was sore,
> Sorrowed for the son she bore;

[6] *Ibid.,* p. 235.
[7] No. XLI is the last of the poems added to the printer's copy of *A Shropshire Lad.* See Haber, *Manuscript Poems,* p. 127.
[8] Stevenson, p. 20.

> And standing hills, long to remain,
> Shared their short-lived comrade's pain.
> And bound for the same bourn as I,
> On every road I wandered by,
> Trod beside me, close and dear,
> The beautiful and death-struck year.
>
> (ll. 1–10)

Yet this closeness to nature—albeit a sorrowing, mortal nature —is absent in London. The persona has lost not only his one-ness with the land but his empathy with man as well:

> Yonder, lightening other loads,
> The seasons range the country roads,
> But here in London streets I ken
> No such helpmates, only men;
> And these are not in plight to bear,
> If they would, another's care.
> They have enough as 'tis: I see
> In many an eye that measures me
> The mortal sickness of a mind
> Too unhappy to be kind.
> Undone with misery, all they can
> Is to hate their fellow man;
> And till they drop they needs must still
> Look at you and wish you ill.
>
> (ll. 19–32)

These lines depict the common pattern of the pastoral exile. To leave the land is to forsake the sympathy which binds man and nature, man and man. On one level, then, the picture of the men of London, who "hate their fellow man," reflects no more than the now-alien vision of the fallen innocent. The world is now perceived as hostile, the homely comforters re-placed by men who "wish you ill."

The contrast between Shropshire and London is continued in two other poems of the exile group. No. LII, "Far in a Western Brookland," echoes the mood of Lyrics XXXVIII–XLI both in its use of wind imagery and its conscious comparison of two distinct states of existence. It too is a vision of the pastoral Eden after the Fall:

> Far in a western brookland
> That bred me long ago
> The poplars stand and tremble
> By pools I used to know.
>
> There, in the windless night-time,
> The wanderer, marvelling why,
> Halts on the bridge to hearken
> How soft the poplars sigh.
>
> He hears: no more remembered
> In fields where I was known,
> Here I lie down in London
> And turn to rest alone.
>
> (ll. 1–12)

The last stanza returns to the image of the wind to suggest the intense existence lost in the departure from Shropshire. The wind which the wanderer hears in the "windless night-time" is the soul of the lad who has forsaken the land of his youth for the barren existence of London:

> There, by the starlit fences,
> The wanderer halts and hears
> My soul that lingers sighing
> About the glimmering weirs.
>
> (ll. 13–16)

Lyric LV is similar in its mood, but it offers a complication to the exile motif, for while the poems of estrangement previously discussed emphasize the loss involved in the transition to London, No. LV suggests that the new existence has also its compensation. It allows the lad to escape one feature which characterized life in Shropshire:

> Westward on the high-hilled plains
> Where for me the world began,
> Still, I think, in newer veins
> Frets the changeless blood of man.

> Now that other lads than I
>   Strip to bathe on Severn shore,
> They, no help, for all they try,
>   Tread the mill I trod before.
>
> (ll. 1–8)

The implication of the last two lines of stanza 2 is that no longer must the London lad "tread the mill [he] trod before." The poem recalls the cycle of change depicted in poems of the Shropshire setting. In fact, the general tone of the Shropshire poems is echoed in the last two stanzas of Lyric LV, which picture youth as a time of uncertainty and change:

> There, when hueless is the west
>   And the darkness hushes wide,
> Where the lad lies down to rest
>   Stands the troubled dream beside.
>
> There, on thoughts that once were mine,
>   Day looks down the eastern steep,
> And the youth at morning shine
>   Makes the vow he will not keep.
>
> (ll. 9–16)

If Shropshire and London are taken as symbolic of two diverse states of existence, it is necessary to recognize that Housman continues in these symbols the central paradox of loss and gain found in the individual poems of *A Shropshire Lad*. The quest for permanence in a mutable world can be achieved only through the sacrifice of the essence of existence itself. But, conversely, the loss of the simplicity and vitality of the pastoral world is partially offset by the more stable vision of maturity. The complex attitude toward life and death, innocence and experience, which is seen in the majority of the poems of *A Shropshire Lad* is paralleled by Housman's treatment of the London exile.

"The Merry Guide," No. XLII, which is a restatement of the journey motif in mythic terms, defines more exactly the symbolism inherent in the movement away from the pastoral

Arcadia. Here the persona recollects the departure from Shropshire not as a train ride "through the wild green hills of Wyre," but, imaginatively, as a mythic journey of death. The merry guide of the poem's title is, as Louise Boas has pointed out, the god Hermes, identified by his feathered cap (stanza 2) and his "serpent-circled wand" (stanza 15).[9] In the poem, Housman brings together many of the symbols used in the preceding exile poems—the journey, the winds, the pastoral Arcadia, and the association of the destination of the journey with death. The choice of Hermes as the guide in the poem seems especially significant. As a classical scholar, Housman knew, of course, that Hermes is the god who guides the dead to Hades; that his birthplace was Arcadia; and that he is the pastoral god, the god of roads, and the protector of travelers.[10] All of these functions are consistent with the images Housman uses in dealing with the departure from Shropshire.

Wind imagery dominates the poem. It opens in "the wind of morning" (l. 1) as the narrator recalls the journey which began as he "ranged the thymy wold" (l. 2). The journey itself is described as the passing of the wind:

> Across the glittering pastures
> And empty upland still
> And solitude of shepherds
> High in the folded hill,
>
> By hanging woods and hamlets
> That gaze through orchards down
> On many a windmill turning
> And far-discovered town,
>
> With gay regards of promise
> And sure unslackened stride

---

[9] "Housman's 'The Merry Guide.' " *Explicator*, III (1944–45), Item 6. See also Tom Burns Haber, *The Making of A Shropshire Lad.* The first draft of the poem bears the Greek subtitle "Hermes, guide of souls," dropped in the second draft.

[10] Miss Boas points out these functions of the god in her analysis of the poem.

> And smiles and nothing spoken
> Led on my merry guide.
> (ll. 21–32)

Like Shelley's west wind, the wind through which the narrator and his guide travel is both "destroyer and preserver,"[11] carrying the blossoms of spring and the dead leaves of autumn. It is a "great gale . . . / That breathes from gardens thinned" (ll. 37–38), and the two travelers are "Borne in the drift of blossoms Whose petals throng the wind" (ll. 39–40). Yet in stanza 13 the two journey through

> . . . the heaven-heard whisper
> Of dancing leaflets whirled
> From all the woods that autumn
> Bereaves in all the world.
> (ll. 49–52)

Thus it is the wind of autumn and of spring, of the destruction of life and of its preservation. It is, in fact, the paradoxical nature of the journey which complicates what is, on the surface, a simple narrative. In stanza 14 the persona perceives that he journeys "midst the fluttering legion / Of all that ever died" (ll. 53–54), yet he follows willingly his "delightful guide."

The characterization of the guide as "delightful" must seem oddly out of place to the reader who realizes that he guides the speaker to the land of the dead. In fact, the title and the description of Hermes all through the poem point up what appears to be the poem's ironical tone. The guide is described in stanza 5 as "my happy guide," and in stanza 8, as in the title, as a "merry guide." In addition, he is characterized in stanza 3 by a "gay delightful guise" and "friendly brows and laughter," and in stanza 5 by "kind looks and laughter," in stanzas 8 and 15 by "gay regards of promise" and "lips that brim with laughter." The persona's depiction of the guide has prompted Louise Boas to call "The Merry Guide" a highly ironic poem:

11 "Ode to the West Wind," l. 14. See also M. H. Abram's discussion of wind imagery in Romantic poetry in *The Mirror and The Lamp* (New York, 1953).

Man might expect this merry guide to lead him to life and love—to Arcadia. But like the trickster he is, he leads man on through the fields and flocks, through the woods and orchards, through sunlight and clouds, to the world of the dead. He makes gay promises—unspoken but implied. A happy journey? So it seems on the surface. But is not the happiness a dream? Hermes is the dream guide. If one follow him then one is in a dream. Man travels then through the dream of life to the reality of death. It is the guide who laughs.[12]

Granted there is an element of irony here, but like other of Housman's titles,[13] the title of this poem is somewhat ambiguous, capable of both a literal and an ironic interpretation. Since, as has been noted in Chapter III, death is itself, like the wind, a preserver and a destroyer, it can be approached both with dread and with rejoicing. "To an Athlete Dying Young" clearly establishes the fact that, at times, death is an occasion of joy rather than of sorrow. The poem, then, may not be as "highly ironic" as Miss Boas has suggested.

"The Merry Guide" has been dated as one of the earliest of the *Shropshire Lad* poems. The first draft bears the notation "Sept. 1890," the first surviving date in the notebooks.[14] And it is significant that the structure of the poem parallels the structure of the entire collection, for "The Merry Guide" suggests that the myth of the journey from the pastoral land was an informing pattern of thought from the earliest stages of composition of the poems of *A Shropshire Lad*. The first stanza is set in Arcadia, where the persona "ranged the thymy wold" and the "brooks ran gold." Hermes, the god of Arcadia, leads him from the "glittering pastures" and the "solitude of shepherds" on a journey which he comes to recognize as a journey of death. The poem begins as a retrospective view of the journey, but during its course the narrator shifts to the present tense, indi-

---

[12] Boas, Item 6.
[13] Compare, for example, "The True Lover" and "The New Mistress."
[14] See Haber, *The Making of A Shropshire Lad*, p. 13.

cating that it continues yet: "We two fare on for ever" (l. 43).
The poem is, in short, the microcosm which mirrors the larger
design of *A Shropshire Lad,* an allegory of the loss of innocence
depicted through the pastoral convention of the departure
from Arcadia.

The implication of "The Merry Guide" is that the departure
leads to a kind of spiritual death,[15] which is also suggested by
the wind symbolism of the early London poems and later by
Lyric LII, in which the persona leaves his soul behind in
Shropshire among the "glimmering weirs." London is, in the
symbolic sense, the hades to which Terence is led by the god of
the dead, corresponding to the "prison-house" of Wordsworth's
"Intimations Ode." Its misery is offset, however, by the further
conceit that this state of spiritual death relieves the lad of some
of the pain of the more vital existence of Shropshire. Employing this conceit, the three poems which follow "The Merry
Guide" in the London sequence deal with the preserving aspect
of death. "The Immortal Part," No. XLIII, pictures man's permanence as beginning after the death of the body and the soul:

> "When shall this slough of sense be cast,
> This dust of thoughts be laid at last,
> The man of flesh and soul be slain
> And the man of bone remain? . . ."
>
> (ll. 5–8)

Lyric XLIV views death as the preserver of man's good name:

Shot? so quick, so clean an ending?

---

15 Because one of the conventions of the pastoral is that an existence close
to the soil, close to nature, is vital and intense, life apart from the pastoral
setting—at court or in the city—involves a loss of this vitality, a complication
of the "simple life," and also a corruption. Poems such as Spenser's *The
Shepheardes Calendar*, Goldsmith's *The Deserted Village*, and Wordsworth's
"Michael" illustrate the persistence of the convention in three different centuries of English poetry. The archetype is seen in the Eden myth of *Paradise
Lost*, where the departure from Milton's pastoral-like Eden symbolizes the
beginning of a mortal state of existence. See also E. B. Greenwood, "Poetry
and Paradise: A Study in Thematics," *Essays in Criticism*, XVII (1967),
6–25.

Oh that was right, lad, that was brave:
Yours was not an ill for mending,
    'Twas best to take it to the grave.

(ll. 1–4)

The paradox of the poem, that to destroy is in one sense to preserve, is continued in the following lyric; and here Housman echoes a Biblical passage to give support to what would otherwise appear a most unorthodox doctrine:

If it chance your eye offend you,
    Pluck it out, lad, and be sound:
'Twill hurt, but here are salves to friend you,
    And many a balsam grows on ground.

And if your hand or foot offend you,
    Cut it off, lad, and be whole;
But play the man, stand up and end you,
    When your sickness is your soul.

The first two lines of stanza 1 recall Christ's words in Matthew 5:29: "And if thy right eye causeth thee to stumble, pluck it out and cast it from thee . . . ." And lines 5 and 6 continue the allusion to verse 30: "And if thy right had causeth thee to stumble, cut it off and cast it from thee: for it is profitable for thee that one of thy members should perish and not thy whole body go into hell." The poet thus justifies an idea that has been bitterly attacked by paraphrasing quite closely a passage from the Sermon on the Mount.

Lyrics XLII–XLV thus complicate the Arcadia-exile pattern by suggesting a more sophisticated view of the process of maturation. Youth, like Shropshire itself, signifies a state of intense feeling for life but also of an increasing anguish over the discovery of decay brought by time. The persona may look back wistfully on the lost youth for which Shropshire now stands, but he finds compensation in the permanence of the symbolic death-state of the London exile, for he has escaped the pain of the youth's first discovery of his own transience. This new direction in thought is exemplified in the later poems of the exile cycle, which deal with the lad's new-found stability, the awakening of a stoicism which quells the "troubled dream" of youth.

One may note, for example, Lyric LI, where the lad sees a Grecian statue in a London gallery. He is "brooding on [his] heavy ill," but the statue is "still in marble stone" and steadfast. He imagines that the statue speaks to him, for he sees that they share a common fate:

> "Well met," I thought the look would say,
> "We both were fashioned far away;
> We neither knew, when we were young,
> These Londoners we live among."
>
> (ll. 7–10)

The statue's imagined advice to the lad is a kind of stoicism: "Courage, lad, 'tis not for long: / Stand, quit you like stone, be strong" (ll. 21–22). The persona, heeding the advice, thus acquires an indifference to pleasure and pain which before was thought to be found only in death. Yet he is able to achieve a degree of permanence in the face of life's transience by adopting the guise of death, becoming a "man of stone":

> And light on me my trouble lay,
> And I stept out in flesh and bone
> Manful like the man of stone.
>
> (ll. 24–26)

Housman's stoicism has been remarked upon frequently, and he has been accused of some inconsistency in adopting such a stance since it contradicts the attitudes expressed in other poems.[16] This apparent inconsistency arises, however, only because the critics have never been careful enough to note the growth and development of the Shropshire lad. It is true, of

---

[16] See Jacob Bronowski, "Alfred Edward Housman" in *The Poet's Defence*, p. 221; and Hugh Molson, "The Philosophies of Hardy and Housman," pp. 207–208. *Stoicism* is used in the popular sense of the word, not as the name of a systematic set of beliefs. The stoicism expressed in Housman's poetry does not represent a philosophy in any strict sense, but an attitude or emotional state.

course, that while many of the poems of the work deal with the pleasures of life at its prime and the simultaneous pain of its dissolution, others voice an unconcern for both its pleasures and its pains. Yet an examination of the position of these poems reveals that the former mood pervades the Shropshire poems; the latter, those poems after the exile. It is not, in fact, until Lyric XLII, "The Merry Guide," that the stoical attitude becomes the dominant tone of the poetry. Earlier poems indeed look forward to death, but only as a means of ending the cycle of endless change.

The mood of the latter poems of *A Shropshire Lad* is that of Lyric XLVIII, to "endure an hour and see injustice done" (l. 12) . The first stanza suggests the futility of struggling against "earth and high heaven":

> Be still, my soul, be still; the arms you bear are brittle,
>   Earth and high heaven are fixt of old and founded strong.
> Think rather,—call to thought, if now you grieve a little,
>   The days when we had rest, O soul, for they were long.
>
>   (ll. 1–4)

The poem also illustrates Housman's ironic use of allusion. Gordon Pitts points out that the poet is echoing and reversing the words of a popular nineteenth-century hymn which begins: "Be still, my soul: The Lord is on thy side; / Bear patiently the cross of grief and pain," and ends:

> Be still, my soul: the hour is hastening on
> When we shall be forever with the Lord,
> When disappointment, grief, and fear are gone.[17]

As Pitts notes, Housman ironically juxtaposes the Christian stoicism of the hymn with his own more naturalistic stoicism.

Lyric XLVI also is concerned with man's impassive reaction to the consequences of his human state. Its conceit is that the appropriate symbols of death are not the green living plants

---

17 "Housman's 'Be Still, My Soul,' " *Victorian Poetry*, III (1965) , 137–38.

which survive the winter and are reborn in the spring. Eternal
Death's proper emblem is "whatever will not flower again":

> Bring, in this timeless grave to throw,
> No cypress, sombre on the snow;
> Snap not from the bitter yew
> His leaves that live December through;
> Break no rosemary, bright with rime
> And sparkling to the cruel clime;
> Nor plod the winter land to look
> For willows in the icy brook
> To cast them leafless round him: bring
> No spray that ever buds in spring.
>
> (ll. 1–10)

The juxtaposition of those plants which survive the winter and
experience the rebirth of spring with the "timeless grave" of
one who "never shall arise" only serves to increase the irony of
man's mortal state. Reflecting a new sense of resignation, the
poem states that man must be comforted by those objects of nature which are for a single season:

> But if the Christmas field has kept
> Awns the last gleaner overstept,
> Or shrivelled flax, whose flower is blue
> A single season, never two;
> Or if one haulm whose year is o'er
> Shivers on the upland frore,
> —Oh, bring from hill and stream and plain
> Whatever will not flower again,
> To give him comfort: he and those
> Shall bide eternal bedfellows
> Where low upon the couch he lies
> Whence he never shall arise.
>
> (ll. 11–22)

Housman depicts in the latter poems of *A Shropshire Lad* an
attitude toward life which seems to follow logically from the
young man's first discovery of his mortality. He offers it not as a

consistent philosophy but as the inevitable emotional response of the man who, cut off from a view of the physical world as permanent and benevolent, cannot accept the existence of a spiritual world which transcends the physical. The young man rebels against the injustice of it all; the mature man accepts the inevitable not as a happy solution but as the only possible one. The new attitude does not relieve the pain, but it renders it bearable. Perhaps the chief distinction of the concluding poems of *A Shropshire Lad* is the evidence of a mature mind imposing order on the flux of experience in a way that the adolescent mind could not. This is not to suggest that the London poems were later in composition, but that Housman's ordering of the work achieves the effect of a persona who grows and matures with the experiences which the poems record.

An example of this maturation is seen in Lyric L, which is the poem of a man who looks back with some insight to the time when he was a Knighton lad:[18]

> In valleys of springs of rivers,
>   By Ony and Teme and Clun,
> The country for easy livers,
>   The quietest under the sun,
>
> We still had sorrows to lighten,
>   One could not be always glad,
> And lads knew trouble at Knighton
>   When I was a Knighton lad.
>
> (ll. 1–8)

Even in youth, he realizes, "one could not be always glad," and if, in London, "sorrow is with one still," it is "small matter for wonder" (ll. 11–12). But if man's burdens increase with age, so does his ability to bear them:

> And if as a lad grows older
>   The troubles he bears are more,

18 Knighton is a town in southwestern Shropshire on the river Teme.

> He carries his griefs on a shoulder
> That handselled them long before.
> (ll. 13–16)

In the imagery of the poem, the pain of human existence is a heavy weight, the luggage which encumbers the journey: "Where shall one halt to deliver / This luggage I'd lief set down?" (ll. 17–18). The poem then looks to a place where this burden may be removed, and the destination is envisaged in the last stanza:

> 'Tis a long way further than Knighton,
> A quieter place than Clun,
> Where doomsday may thunder and lighten
> And little 'twill matter to one.
> (ll. 21–24)

The pun on *lighten* in line 23 suggests the basis for the poem's stoical view that the thunder of doomsday will "little . . . matter to one," for two senses of *lighten* are meaningful in the context of the poem: "to shine like lightning," and "to relieve of a load."

The concluding poems of *A Shropshire Lad* thus depict, on the whole, the mood of one who is resigned to the fact of death and has lost the frustration of the youth who first becomes aware that he must die. Anguish is replaced by nostalgia for lost youth and, especially towards the end of the work, for friends the persona has outlived. "With Rue My Heart Is Laden," No. LIV, is perhaps the finest expression of this mood, but other less successful poems voice the same sentiment. Lyric LVIII mourns "two honest lads" who accompanied the lad when he "came last to Ludlow," and "The Isle of Portland," No. LIX, mourns the loss of a friend:

> On yonder island, not to rise,
> Never to stir forth free,
> Far from his folk a dead lad lies
> That once was friends with me.
> (ll. 5–8)

Finally, "Hughley Steeple," No. LXI and the last of the poems within the frame, is concerned wholly with the death of friends whom the lad has survived:

> The vane on Hughley steeple
> Veers bright, a far-known sign,
> And there lie Hughley people,
> And there lie friends of mine.
> Tall in their midst the tower
> Divides the shade and sun,
> And the clock strikes the hour
> And tells the time to none.
>
> (ll. 1–8)

The pattern of the poem's imagery is controlled by Hughley steeple itself, which divides the shade and sun, the north and the south. These two locations take on special significance, for the shaded northern side contains the suicides:

> To south the headstones cluster,
> The sunny mounds lie thick;
> The dead are more in muster
> At Hughley than the quick.
> North, for a soon-told number,
> Chill graves the sexton delves,
> And steeple-shadowed slumber
> The slayers of themselves.
>
> (ll. 9–16)

The narrator, resigned to death, makes no distinction between the groups. Death is now a matter of indifference:

> To north, to south, lie parted,
> With Hughley tower above,
> The kind, the single-hearted,
> The lads I used to love.
> And, south or north, 'tis only
> A choice of friends one knows,
> And I shall ne'er be lonely
> Asleep with these or those.
>
> (ll. 17–24)

On the surface, "Hughley Steeple" may appear to violate the Shropshire-exile structure, since its setting is Shropshire. Yet there is nothing in the poem to suggest that the speaker is now in Shropshire viewing the scene he is describing. A number of the concluding poems are, in effect, the recollections of Shropshire scenes and landmarks. The nature of the description of Hughley steeple itself justifies such a reading, for the poem reconstructs not so much a specific scene described in detail as a pattern such as the mind imposes on the scene half-remembered, the tower neatly dividing the cemetery between sun and shade. Hughley steeple is, moreover, a "far-known sign," a famous landmark which would be apt to be recalled to the consciousness of one who has left it. This interpretation is supported also by the fact that the speaker refers to the scene as *there,* not *here*: "And there lie Hughley people, / And there lie friends of mine" (ll. 3–4). Finally, it may be pointed out that in other poems of the London group the narrator described scenes in Shropshire as if he were actually present, though obviously he was not. Lyric LII pictures a scene in "a western brookland" where "poplars stand and tremble" and a wanderer "halts on the bridge to hearken / How soft the poplars sigh." At the conclusion of the poem, however, it is made clear that this scene is viewed only in the imagination, for the narrator says of himself: "Here I lie down in London / And turn to rest alone."

Of the twenty-five poems of the exile cycle, only three others suggest a rural scene in possible violation of the Shropshire-London ordering. "The True Lover" and "The Carpenter's Son" imply indirectly such a setting, but the words of the young rustics of both poems are enclosed in quotation marks to distinguish the speakers from Terence, the persona of the vast majority of the poems. It may be that the two were grouped with the exile poems because they depict the stoical acceptance of death which is characteristic of the London cycle. In any case, Housman separates them from the cycle of Terence poems with his punctuation. Lyric LVIII, however, presents a problem of a different sort. The poem is as follows:

When I came last to Ludlow
　　Amidst the moonlight pale,
Two friends kept step beside me,
　　Two honest lads and hale.

Now Dick lies long in the churchyard,
　　And Ned lies long in jail,
And I come home to Ludlow
　　Amidst the moonlight pale.

Obviously a long absence from the Shropshire setting is depicted, since Dick, who "lies long in the churchyard," was with
the narrator when he last visited Ludlow. But the poem does
not state that he has returned, only that he is in the act of returning or anticipates returning. In common usage the present
tense of the verb carries with it the idea of futurity. "I go now"
implies "I shall go" or "I am about to go." Coming as it does
at the conclusion of *A Shropshire Lad*, Lyric LVIII merely
echoes the resignation of all the concluding poems of the work.
The lad is preparing to join his lost friends at Ludlow, sym-
bolically to meet death, just as in "Hughley Steeple" he is will-
ing to accept the fate of those who lie in the graves of Hughley
cemetery. Whatever the actual setting of the poem, however,
it clearly belongs to the exile phase of the speaker's life, and its
sense of resignation is exactly that of the two poems placed be·
tween "When I Came Last to Ludlow" and "Hughley Steeple."
Both poems image the approach of oblivious death as the
fall of darkness:

Now hollow fires burn out to black,
　　And lights are guttering low:
Square your shoulders, lift your pack,
　　And leave your friends and go.

Oh never fear, man, nought's to dread,
　　Look not left nor right:
In all the endless road you tread
　　There's nothing but the night.
　　　　　　　　　　　(Lyric LX)

The lad's response to a fate which now seems imminent is that
of the "man of stone":

> Lie you easy, dream you light,
> And sleep you fast for aye;
> And luckier may you find the night
> Than ever you found the day.
> (Lyric LIX, ll. 9–12)

The concluding poems thus signal an end to the cycle which
began with the sunrise of "Reveille" awakening the young man
to "feast his heart" on a world at its prime, and one indication
of the gulf which lies between the final poems of *A Shropshire
Lad* and those which initiate the cycle may be seen in the contrasting imagery of the two groups. The cherry trees and daf-
fodils of the opening lyrics, the images of dawn and of spring,
are far removed from the graveyards and the darkness of
Lyrics LVIII–LXI. The sun has run its course from dawn to
dusk, and if the sunshine of the early Shropshire poems is a
"glorious birth," the setting sun of the final lyrics takes "a so-
ber coloring from an eye / That hath kept watch o'er man's
mortality." That the progression of Housman's imagery should
recall that of Wordsworth's "Intimations Ode" is perhaps inevitable, for Housman too is concerned with the loss of a harmony with nature found only in the innocent's vision of the
world. Furthermore, he deals, as does Wordsworth, with the
"ages" of man, and the changing response to the external
world which these ages bring. But for Housman's persona the
recollections of early childhood bring only intimations of mortality, and it is primarily with these death-thoughts that the
exile poems conclude. The philosophic mind which is in evidence in the latter stages of *A Shropshire Lad* is not based on
a Wordsworthian intimation of nature's divinity but on an
acceptance of the fact of man's essential mortality and a view
of death which makes it—at least in the logic of poetic conceit
—not merely destructive.

Yet, like Wordsworth's child, who is "father of the man," Housman's Shropshire lad undergoes a process which takes him from innocence to knowledge (and anguish) and, finally, to resignation. It is a paradoxical process and not one upon which a consistent philosophy ought to be based, but as Housman himself reminds us in a discussion of Wordsworth, "Poetry is no matter of fundamental tenets. . . ."[19] The thematic and structural unity of *A Shropshire Lad* has its basis in the emotional and imaginative response of man to the elementary facts of his existence. Its order is not logical in the strict sense of the word, but archetypal, which may explain, in part, why critics who have continued to regard Housman's poetry as a kind of philosophy have failed to discern any evidence of thematic design in *A Shropshire Lad*.

[19] See Housman's review of *The Cambridge History of English Literature,* Vol. IX: "The Period of the French Revolution," in *A. E. Housman: Selected Prose*, ed. by John Carter, p. 112.

VIII

THE NAME AND NATURE OF
HOUSMAN'S POETRY

*1*t is ironic, in view of Housman's own conception of the business of criticism, that his poetry should have suffered its present fate of being subordinated to the critics' preoccupation with extra-literary matters. Housman wrote in 1915 while reviewing a study of the English literature of the period of the French Revolution, "Now the centre of interest in a poet is his poetry: not his themes, his doctrines, his opinions, his life or conduct, but the poetical quality of the works he has bequeathed to us."[1] It was decided, however, soon after Housman's death, or perhaps before, that there was very little to be said about the poetical quality of his simple verse, and that criticism must be content with his life, his opinions and doctrines, and, to a lesser extent, his themes. But, in truth, much remains to be said about the poetical quality of the works he has bequeathed to us. What, specifically, is the nature of Housman's art and of his achievement as a poet?

First, one must consider seriously the matter of his infamous "simplicity." The preceding pages have suggested that the artless, uncomplicated manner of Housman's verse is more apparent than real. His poetry is not entirely free from punning and a certain ambiguity of statement. It is characterized to a

[1] This quotation appears in the review of *The Cambridge History of English Literature*, IX: "The Period of the French Revolution," reprinted in *A. E. Housman: Selected Prose*, pp. 108–14.

greater extent by conceit, paradox, irony—in short, the qualities which have been viewed by much modern criticism as the marks of a necessary complexity in poetic texture. Added to these devices is a use of allusion that one might well call modern. Housman's allusive technique frequently serves to complicate the seemingly simple statement of a poem by echoing and reversing a commonplace expression or a passage from another work so that the resulting tone is a complex one. This statement is not to imply that Housman is "modern" in any real sense, only that his directness is often a matter of metrical form and of the tradition of the pastoral and the ballad, as distinguished from a threadbare texture. It is the subtlety with which Housman employs these techniques that suggests a distinction between his poetry and that of the moderns. It may also help to account for the fact that his ironies have been mistaken for literal statement, his paradoxes for perversity, and his conceits for personal belief.

But in spite of his use of many of the devices of wit, Housman's poetic mode is more akin to the Romantic tradition than to the modern.[2] Wordsworth he considered "the chief figure in English poetry after Chaucer," and he declared that "no poet later born . . . entirely escaped his influence."[3] Whether he considered Wordsworth a strong influence on his own poetry will never be known; Housman was not given to discussions of his art. But it is nevertheless true that his verse owes much to the tradition of Wordsworth. This debt is manifested not only in the rural setting and the pastoral persona, but in such persistent themes as the city-country antithesis, the loss of harmony with nature, and the nostalgia for lost innocence. John Stevenson, who locates the roots of Housman's lyric tradition in romanticism, states:

> Housman's use of a pastoral setting and his adoption of
> the character of the "lad" are part of the same motive

[2] Housman's relationship to the Romantic tradition has been discussed by John Stevenson, "Housman's Lyric Tradition," pp. 17–21.

[3] Carter, *Selected Prose*, p. 109.

which sent Wordsworth to the simple character and the bucolic setting; and while the Shropshire lad is not Peter Bell or Michael, just as he is not Nick Adams or Jake Barnes, he is nevertheless the type of innocent, the young man in search of being in an alien world; he is the youth confronted with the discovery of the knowledge of good and evil.[4]

One might go even further to suggest that Housman's conception of the nature of poetry was essentially Romantic. His lecture on "The Name and Nature of Poetry" offers the doctrine that poetry is "more physical than intellectual."[5] He describes the process by which his own poetry came into being as follows:

> Having drunk a pint of beer at luncheon—beer is a sedative to the brain, and my afternoons are the least intellectual portion of my life—I would go out for a walk of two or three hours. As I went along, thinking of nothing in particular, only looking at things around me and following the progress of the seasons, there would flow into my mind, with sudden and unaccountable emotion, sometimes a line or two of verse, sometimes a whole stanza at once, accompanied, not preceded, by a vague notion of the poem which they were destined to form part of. Then there would usually be a lull of an hour or so, then perhaps the spring would bubble up again.[6]

Housman describes here nothing less than Wordsworth's well-known "spontaneous overflow of powerful feelings," and he clearly recognized it as such, for he quotes Wordsworth's definition as evidence that "other poetry came into existence in the same way"[7]

4 Stevenson, "Housman's Lyric Tradition," p. 19. One might add that if the Shropshire lad is not Michael, he is more nearly Michael's son Luke, who in Wordsworth's "Pastoral Poem" leaves the Sheepfold for the "dissolute city." See "Michael," ll. 382–447.

5 Carter, *Selected Prose*, p. 193.

6 *Ibid.*, p. 194.

7 *Ibid.*, p. 193.

One would not wish, however, to push Housman's debt to the tradition of Wordsworth too far. If he owed something of his lyric impulse to the Romantics, he also disavowed the Romantic doctrine of nature and the essentially spiritual view of the universe as a force in harmony with man's own nature. It is Housman's post-Darwinian conception of the natural world that alienates him from the Romantics and allies him with the moderns, so that, finally, his poetry lies between two traditions, one defunct, the other not yet fully developed. And his unique position in the history of nineteenth- and twentieth-century English poetry explains, in part, the failure of scholarship to do justice to a poetry which combines the simple lyricism of one tradition with the complex attitudes of another.

But even if Housman anticipated to some degree the course of English literature, his work failed to influence the direction that poetry was to take in the twentieth century. He remains a minor figure whose fame rests on the solid achievement of one volume of poems. Furthermore, he has suffered the fate, as Ian Scott-Kilvert notes, of "a minor poet thrust by popularity into the role of a major one."[8] The suspicion persists that the popular poet is, at best, second rate; but Housman's achievement, however minor, deserves to be more correctly assessed.

Such a reassessment must begin with the recognition of the art of *A Shropshire Lad*. It has long been regarded as a collection of short lyrics which voice a *fin de siècle* pessimism. But *A Shropshire Lad* is clearly more than a collection; it is unified in theme and tone, and its force derives from the effect of the whole work, not merely from isolated lyrics. Housman was undoubtedly correct in prohibiting during his lifetime the divorcing of individual poems from their context, for the modern practice of excerpting single poems from *A Shropshire Lad* for anthologies has obscured the essential unity of the work. It has also obscured the fact that, thematically and structurally, *A Shropshire Lad* is a self-contained work, a factor that has some implications for Housman scholarship.

8 *A. E. Housman*, p. 37.

It means, in short, that scholars must turn from Housman's life to his art in seeking to explain the nature of his achievement as a poet. For example, the dramatis personae of *A Shropshire Lad*—the soldier, the young sinner, the forsaken lover, the rustic—may be defined more exactly in terms of the over-all thematic design of the work than in terms of the personal inadequacies of the poet. No one would deny the value of biographical and historical scholarship; but after it has finished its task, the aesthetic problems of a work of art remain untouched, a fact of which Housman scholarship serves as the classic example.

The problem is illustrated by the question of the ordering of the poems of *A Shropshire Lad*. A number of early reviewers detected a consistent order in the arrangement of the poems, but in the last twenty years no one has examined the work closely from this point of view. Professor Haber has attempted to solve the problem of the ordering of the poems by reference to Housman's notebooks and his "nature," not by an analysis of the finished work. He found, as might be expected, that the notebooks do not yield any evidence of a thematic arrangement, and he further states:

> Such problems as order and climax, the building up of tonal effects, nuance, and resolution did not present themselves significantly to Housman. These things came to him easily if they came at all, a part of the largesse of the afternoon's walk. When brain had to settle down to the task of putting the stanzas of a poem in order, trouble usually arose. On a larger scale, in his gathering of the sixty-three poems of his first book, it would have been contrary to Housman's nature to concern himself with any but the elementary matters of arrangement and grouping of his lyrics.[9]

This is surely a dangerous line of argument. To contend that it was "contrary to Housman's nature" to give order to his art is to question seriously his abilities as an artist. But perhaps even more difficult to accept is the implication that our knowl-

[9] *The Making of a Shropshire Lad*, p. 22.

edge of the character of a poet is ample evidence of the kind of work he will produce.

The evidence of the notebooks is that the composition of the individual poems preceded the ordering of the whole. Yet the evidence of the finished work, viewed as a whole, is that its structure is functional in reinforcing the pervasive theme of the poems. One must conclude that at some point between the composition of the earliest of the lyrics before 1890 and the publication of *A Shropshire Lad* in 1896, Housman's critical insight began to work on the product of his poetic sensibility. The alterations in the printer's copy of *A Shropshire Lad* are evidence that the poet was indeed concerned with the ordering of his poems. But any meaningful answer to the problem of the structure of *A Shropshire Lad* must come ultimately from an examination of the finished work itself.

If the work does reveal some evidence of order, what is the nature of that order? The structure of *A Shropshire Lad* is narrative only as far as it involves a clearly defined persona, the record of his discoveries of the nature of his world, and his journey from the place of his birth to the alien city. By far the most significant structural elements are thematic. That is, one may identify in the work, as it is ordered, the growth and development of one predominant theme which corresponds to a configuration of emotion or feeling in the mind of the persona. What has not been recognized is that the theme evident in the individual lyrics is reinforced by the structure of the work as a whole.

Evidence of this structural pattern can be noted, first of all, in the frame poems. The introductory poem and the final two lyrics of the work are important to the design of the whole by virtue of the fact that they define and clarify the purpose and scope of *A Shropshire Lad*. Through allusions to another poetic tradition, these poems provide the necessary context for Housman's own treatment of one of the most pervasive themes of Western literature. Furthermore, Housman uses this framework to justify the theme and tone of his poetry and to suggest its ultimate value. This structural element of *A Shropshire Lad* is too obvious to have been completely overlooked, and even Haber admits that the "appropriateness of 'I hoed and trenched and weeded' to be the final poem is beyond dispute."[10]

But it is difficult to accept the notion that Housman carefully ordered one portion of his work and gathered the remaining lyrics indiscriminately. Even though his account of the genesis of the individual poems implies a doctrine of spontaneous and passive creativity, it must not be forgotten that Housman was not only a poet but an editor and critic as well. It has been traditionally held that Housman represents the classic case of the bifurcation of emotion and intellect,[11] an argument that is supported by his own statements on the divergent nature of poetry and criticism. Yet it is impossible to conceive of the complete separation of the two faculties, even in a man who attempted throughout his career to divorce his poetry from his scholarship. How could the classical scholar avoid seeing the potentialities of the genre which informed his work? The pastoral tradition provided the conventions for unifying the separate poems, which were themselves the product of the union of classical learning and personal insight. If, in Housman's theory of poetics, creation is, on the whole, a passive process and an end in itself, he also held that the business of the critic is to impose order on that which is created. Furthermore, Housman never held that his art was entirely divorced from his intellectual faculties. Although, he says, a poem may have originated as a purely emotional activity, sometimes it "had to be taken in hand and completed by the brain. . . ."[12]

One might well conjecture that this was the process of *A Shropshire Lad*. The individual lyrics began as "secretions"

[10] *Ibid.*, p. 23.
[11] See Brooks Otis, "Housman and Horace," *Pacific Coast Philology*, II (1967), 5–24, for a statement of this view of Housman.
[12] Carter, *Selected Prose*, p. 195.

of emotions, to use Housman's own terminology; but when this activity was done and the poet was faced with the task of arranging the poems for publication, they "had to be taken in hand and completed by the brain." This is perhaps the simplest explanation for the consistency of the structure of *A Shropshire Lad*—the Shropshire-London arrangement, the pattern of growth and knowledge evident in the persona of the poems, and the final resolution of the theme. But to conjecture about the poet's process of creation is dangerous. The most that one can conclude is that the view of *A Shropshire Lad* as an ordered whole is not as inconsistent with Housman's nature and his doctrine of poetry as earlier criticism has suggested.

Housman's theory of the name and nature of poetry does, however, cast some light on the lasting appeal of his art. He held that the ultimate strength of poetry lies in the fact that it deals with unconscious, archetypal patterns of thought and feeling. He states, for example, that the words of a poem "find their way to something in man which is obscure and latent, something older than the present organization of his nature, like the patches of fen which still linger here and there in the drained lands of Cambridgeshire."[13] And he repeated as praiseworthy a statement made about Wordsworth: "his indisputable sovereignty . . . lies in his extraordinary faculty of giving utterance to some of the most elementary and at the same time obscure sensations of man confronted by natural phenomena."[14] One might amend this statement to suggest one reason for the continued appeal of a work which, by all rights, should not have survived far into the twentieth century. Clearly, a part of Housman's achievement as a poet was to give coherence to the elementary and obscure sensations of man confronted by natural phenomena, but these phenomena reveal that the Wordsworthian affinity with nature has been lost; what remains is the realization of the transience and mortality of an essentially alien world.

[13] *Ibid.,* p. 193.
[14] *Ibid.,* p. 113.

SELECTED BIBLIOGRAPHY

Abel, Darrel. "Housman's 'The True Lover,' " *Explicator,* VIII (1949–50), Item 23.

Abrams, M. H. *The Mirror and The Lamp.* New York: Norton, 1953.

Aiken, Conrad. "A. E. Housman," *New Republic,* LXXXIX (November 11, 1936), 51–52.

Alden, Raymond M. "The Lyrical Conceit of the Elizabethans," *Studies in Philology,* XIV (1917), 129–52.

Aldington, Richard. "A. E. Housman" in *A. E. Housman and W. B. Yeats.* Hurst, Berkshire: The Peacock Press, 1955, pp. 5–19.

Allison, A. F. "The Poetry of A. E. Housman," *Review of English Studies,* XIX (1943), 276–84.

Andrews, S. G. "Housman's 'The Carpenter's Son,' " *Explicator,* XIX (1960–61), Item 3.

Anonymous. "Housman's 'The Deserter,' " *Notes and Queries,* V (1958), 258–60.

Bache, William. "Housman's 'To an Athlete Dying Young,' " *Explicator,* X (1951–52), Item 6.

Benét, William Rose. "The Passion for Perfection," *Saturday Review of Literature,* XXIX (February 2, 1946), 10–11.

———. "A. E. Housman's 'Last Poems,' " *Bookman,* LVII (1923), 85.

Bishop, John Peale. "The Poetry of A. E. Housman," *Poetry,* LVI (1940), 144–53.

Blackmur, R. P. *The Expense of Greatness.* Gloucester, Massachusetts: Peter Smith, 1958.

Boas, Louise. "Housman's 'The Merry Guide,' " *Explicator,* III (1944–45), Item 6.

Bowra, C. M. "The Scholarship of A. E. Housman," *Spectator,* CLVI (June 19, 1936), 1137.

Brannin, James. "Alfred Housman," *Sewanee Review,* XXXIII (1925), 191–98.

Brenner, Rica. "Alfred Edward Housman" in *Ten Modern Poets.* New York: Harcourt, Brace, 1930, pp. 175–92.

Bronowski, Jacob. "Alfred Edward Housman" in *The Poet's Defence.* Cambridge: University Press, 1939, pp. 209–28.

Brooks, Benjamin G. "A. E. Housman's Collected Poetry," *Nineteenth Century,* CXXVIII (1940), 71–76.

Brooks, Cleanth. "The Whole of Housman," *Kenyon Review,* III (1941), 105–109.

———. "Housman's '1887,' " *Explicator,* II (1943–44), Item 34.

———. *The Well Wrought Urn.* New York: Harcourt, Brace, 1947.

———. "Alfred Edward Housman," *Anniversary Lectures 1959,* The Library of Congress, 1959, pp. 39–56.

———, and Robert Penn Warren. *Understanding Poetry.* New York: Henry Holt, 1938, pp. 384–87.

———, et al. *An Approach to Literature.* New York: F. S. Crofts, 1952.

Brown, Stuart Gerry. "The Poetry of A. E. Housman," *Sewanee Review,* XLVIII (1940), 397–408.

Burdett, Osbert. *The Beardsley Period.* London: John Lane, 1925.

Bush, Douglas, ed., *The Complete Poetical Works of John Milton.* Boston: Houghton Mifflin, 1965.

Campbell, Harry M. "Conflicting Metaphors: A Poem by A. E. Housman," *CEA Critic,* XXII (1960), 4.

Carter, John. "The Text of Housman's Poems," *Times Literary Supplement* (June 15, 1956), 361.

————. "Missing Housman Manuscripts," *Times Literary Supplement* (December 7, 1962) , 984.

Chambers, R. W. "A. E. Housman" in *Man's Unconquerable Mind*. Philadelphia: Albert Saifer, 1953, pp. 365–86.

Clemens, Cyril. *An Evening with A. E. Housman*. Webster Grove, Missouri: Webster Printing Company, 1937.

————. "Some Unpublished Housman Letters," *Poet Lore*, LIII (1947) , 255–62.

Cockerell, Sir Sydney. "Dates of Housman Poems," *Times Literary Supplement* (November 7, 1936) , 908. Reprinted in Grant Richards, *Housman 1897–1936*. New York: Oxford University Press, 1942, pp. 436–37.

Collins, H. P. *Modern Poetry*. London: Jonathan Cape, 1925.

Colum, Mary M. "Poets and Psychologists," *Forum*, CIII (1940) , 322–23.

Combellack, C. R. B. "Housman's 'To an Athlete Dying Young,'" *Explicator*, X (1951–52) , Item 31.

Connolly, Cyril. "A. E. Housman: A Controversy" in *The Condemned Playground*. New York: Macmillan, 1946, pp. 47–63.

Dean-Smith, Margaret. "Housman's 'The Deserter,'" *Notes and Queries*, IX (1962) , 275–76.

Dobrée, Bonamy. "The Complete Housman," *Spectator*, CLXIV (January 5, 1940) , 22–23.

Dudley, Fred A. "Housman's 'Terence, This Is Stupid Stuff,'" *Explicator*, XIV (1955–56) , Item 2.

Editors of *Explicator*. "Housman's 'Loveliest of Trees,'" *Explicator*, I (1942–43) , Item 57.

Ehrsam, Theodore. *A Bibliography of Alfred Edward Housman*. Boston: Faxton, 1941.

Eliot, T. S. *The Waste Land and Other Poems*. New York: Harcourt, Brace, 1962.

Empson, William. *Some Versions of Pastoral*. Norfolk, Connecticut: New Directions, 1960.

Evans, B. I. *English Poetry in the Later Nineteenth Century*. London: Methuen, 1933.

Fletcher, G. B. A. "On Housman Lucretiana," *Classical Journal*, LIV (1958), 171.

———. "Notes on Housman's Poetry" in Grant Richards, *Housman 1897–1936*. New York: Oxford University Press, 1942, pp. 399–435.

Frye, Northrop. *The Educated Imagination*. Bloomington: Indiana University Press, 1964.

———. "Archetypal Criticism: Theory of Myths" in *Anatomy of Criticism*. Princeton: Princeton University Press, 1957.

Franklin, Ralph. "Housman's Shropshire," *Modern Language Quarterly*, XXIV (1963), 164–71.

Freimarck, Vincent. "Further Notes on Housman's Use of the Bible," *Modern Language Notes*, LXVII (1952), 548–550.

Fuquay, Albert. "A Study of the Criticism of the Poetry of A. E. Housman," an unpublished thesis, University of Florida, 1948.

Garrod, H. W. "Mr. A. E. Housman" in *The Profession of Poetry and Other Lectures*. Oxford: Clarendon Press, 1929, pp. 211–24.

———. "Housman: 1939," *Essays and Studies*, XXV (1939), 7–21.

Ghiselin, Brewster. "Housman's 'The Oracles,' " *Explicator*, IX (1950–51), Item 33.

Gorman, Herbert S. "Hardy and Housman" in *The Procession of Masks*. Boston: B. J. Brimmer Company, 1923, pp. 171–83.

Gosse, Edmund. "A Shropshire Lad" in *More Books on the Table*. London: William Heinemann, 1923, pp. 19–27.

Gow, A. S. F. *A. E. Housman: A Sketch Together with a List of His Writings and Indexes to His Classical Papers*. New York: Macmillan, 1936.

Graves, Robert. *On English Poetry*. London: William Heinemann, 1922.

Greenwood, E. B. "Poetry and Paradise: A Study in Thematics," *Essays in Criticism*, XVII (1967), 6–25.

Griffith, Ben W. "Housman's 'Terence, This Is Stupid Stuff,' " *Explicator*, XIII (1954–55), Item 16.

Gross, Seymour L. "Housman and Pindar," *Notes and Queries,* IV (1957), 128–29.

Haber, Tom Burns. "The Spirit of the Perverse in A. E. Housman," *South Atlantic Quarterly,* XL (1941), 368–78.

————. "The Influence of the Ballads in Housman's Poetry," *Studies in Philology,* XXXIX (1942), 118–29.

————. "Heine and Housman," *Journal of English and Germanic Philology,* XLIII (1944), 326–32.

————. "What Fools These Mortals Be: Housman's Poetry and the Lyrics of Shakespeare," *Modern Language Quarterly,* VI (1945), 499–58.

————. "Housman's Poetic Ear," *Poet Lore,* LIV (1948), 257–69.

————. "The Poetic Antecedents of A. E. Housman's 'Hell Gate,'" *Philological Quarterly,* XXXI (1952), 433–36.

————. "How 'Poetic' is A. E. Housman's Poetry?" *Modern Language Notes,* LXVII (1952), 551–52.

————. "Housman's 'Now Hollow Fires Burn Out to Black,'" *Explicator,* XI (1952–53), Item 35.

————. "Housman's Poetic Method: His Lecture and His Notebooks," *PMLA,* LXIX (1954), 1000–1016.

————. "A. E. Housman's Downward Eye," *Journal of English and Germanic Philology,* LIII (1954), 306–18.

————. "A. E. Housman: Astronomer-Poet," *English Studies,* XXXV (1954), 154–58.

————. "Parallels in Juvenal and Housman," *Classical Journal,* LII (1956), 123–24.

————. "A. E. Housman and *Ye Rounde Table,*" *Journal of English and Germanic Philology,* LXI (1962), 797–809.

————. "Housman and Lucretius," *Classical Journal,* LVIII (1963), 173–82.

————. *The Making of a Shropshire Lad.* Seattle: The University of Washington Press, 1966.

————. "A. E. Housman and Coventry Patmore," *CEA Critic,* XXVIII (1966), 9, 11–12.

————. *The Manuscript Poems of A. E. Housman*. Minneapolis: The University of Minnesota Press, 1955.

————. *A. E. Housman*. New York: Twayne, 1967.

Harding, Davis P. "A Note on Housman's Use of the Bible," *Modern Language Notes*, LXV (1950), 205–207.

Harper, George McLean. "Hardy, Hudson, Housman," *Scribner's Magazine*, LXXVIII (1925), 151–57.

Hawkins, Maude. *A. E. Housman: Man Behind a Mask*. Chicago: H. Regnery, 1958.

————. "Housman's 'The True Lover,'" *Explicator*, VIII (1949–50), Item 61.

Henry, Nat. "Housman's 'To an Athlete Dying Young,'" *Explicator*, XII (1953–54), Item 48.

Housman, Alfred Edward. *A Shropshire Lad*, ed. by Carl J. Weber. Waterville, Maine: Colby College Library, 1946.

————. *Selected Prose*, ed. by John Carter. New York: Cambridge University Press, 1961.

Housman, Laurence. *The Unexpected Years*. New York: Bobbs-Merrill, 1936.

————. *My Brother, A. E. Housman: Personal Recollections Together with Thirty Hitherto Unpublished Poems*. New York: Charles Scribner's Sons, 1938.

Hyder, Clyde K. "Housman's 'The Oracles,'" *Explicator*, IV (1945–46), Item 5.

————. "Housman's 'Her Strong Enchantments Failing,'" *Explicator*, IV (1945–46), Item 11.

Jackson, Holbrook. "The Poetry of A. E. Housman," *Living Age*, CCCII (September 20, 1919), 728–31.

Jarrell, Randall. "Texts from Housman," *Kenyon Review*, I (1939), 260–70.

Johnson, H. Harrold. "A. E. Housman: Poet and Pessimist," *Hibbert Journal*, XXXV (1937), 380–90.

Kane, Robert J. "Housman's 'Terence, This Is Stupid Stuff,'" *Explicator*, X (1951–52), Query 7.

Kowalczyk, R. L. "Horatian Tradition and Pastoral Mode in

Housman's *A Shropshire Lad,*" *Victorian Poetry,* IV (1966),
223–35.

Kronenberger, Louis. "A Note on A. E. Housman," *Nation,*
CXLV (December 18, 1937), 690–91.

Leggett, B. J. "Housman's 'The Recruit,'" *Explicator,* XXV
(1965–66), Item 25.

———. "The Miltonic Allusions in Housman's 'Terence, This
Is Stupid Stuff,'" *English Language Notes,* V (1968), 202–
207.

———. "An Unpublished Housman Letter on the Preface to
Last Poems," *Victorian Newsletter,* XXXIII (1968), 48–49.

Leighton, Lawrence. "One View of Housman," *Poetry,* LII
(1938), 94–100.

LeMire, Eugene D. "The Irony and Ethics of *A Shropshire
Lad,*" *University of Windsor Review,* I (1965), 109–27.

Lucas, F. L. *The Decline and Fall of the Romantic Ideal.* New
York: Macmillan, 1937.

———. "A. E. Housman's Poetry," *New Statesman and Nation,*
XI (May 30, 1936), 854.

Lynskey, Winifred. "Housman's 'Loveliest of Trees,'" *Explicator,* IV (1945–46), Item 59.

———. "A Critic in Action: Mr. Ransom," *College English,* V
(1944), 240–49.

Macdonald, J. F. "The Poetry of A. E. Housman," *Queen's
Quarterly,* XXXI (1923), 114–37.

Macklem, Michael. "The Elegiac Theme in Housman," *Queen's
Quarterly,* LIX (1952), 39–52.

MacNeice, Louis. *The Poetry of W. B. Yeats.* New York: Oxford
University Press, 1941.

———. "Housman in Retrospect," *New Republic,* CII (April
29, 1940), 583.

Marlow, Norman. *A. E. Housman: Scholar and Poet.* Minneapolis: The University of Minnesota Press, 1958.

Marshall, George O. "A Miltonic Echo in Housman," *Notes
and Queries,* New Series, V (1958), 258.

Martin, Houston. "With Letters from Housman," *Yale Review*, XXVI (1936), 283–303.

Maurer, K. W. "A. E. Housman, Postuma," *Anglia*, LXIII (1939), 197–208.

Miles, Josephine. "The Pathetic Fallacy and the Thing in Itself," *Poetry*, LXIII (1944), 210–18.

Molson, Hugh. "The Philosophies of Hardy and Housman," *Quarterly Review*, CCLXVIII (1937), 205–13.

Monro, Harold. *Some Contemporary Poets (1920)*. London: Leonard Parsons, 1920.

Morse, J. Mitchell. "Housman: A Cautionary Note," *Notes and Queries*, I (1954), 449–50.

Mortimer, Raymond. "Housman's Relics," *New Statesman and Nation*, XII (October 24, 1936), 631, 634.

Mounts, Charles E. "Housman's Twisting of Scripture," *Modern Language Notes*, LXI (1946), 186.

Muir, Edwin. "A. E. Housman," *London Mercury*, XXXV (1936), 62–63.

Myers, Walter L. "Housman's 'To an Athlete Dying Young,'" *Explicator*, XI (1952–53), Item 23.

Nitchie, Elizabeth. "Housman's 'To an Athlete Dying Young,'" *Explicator*, X (1951–52), Item 57.

Oliver, F. W. "A. E. Housman: Some Recollections" in Grant Richards, *Housman 1897–1936*. New York: Oxford University Press, 1942, pp. 438–40.

Otis, Brooks. "Housman and Horace," *Pacific Coast Philology*, II (1967), 5–24.

Pearsall, Robert Brainard. "Housman Versus Vaughan Williams: 'Is My Team Plowing?'" *Victorian Poetry*, IV (1966), 42–44.

————. "The Vendible Values of Housman's Soldiery," *PMLA*, LXXXII (1967), 85–90.

Peterson, Spiro. "Housman's 'On Wenlock Edge,'" *Explicator*, XV (1956–57), Item 46.

Phelps, William Lyon. *The Advance of English Poetry in the*

Twentieth Century. New York: Dodd, Mead and Company, 1924

Pitts, Gordon, "Housman's 'Be Still, My Soul,' " *Victorian Poetry*, III (1965), 137–38.

Pollet, Maurice. "Lettre inédite de A. E. Housman," *Etudes Anglaises*, V (1937), 403–04.

Pound, Ezra. "Mr. Housman at Little Bethel," *Criterion*, XIII (1934), 216–224.

Priestley, J. B. "The Poetry of A. E. Housman," *London Mercury*, VII (1922), 171–84.

R. T. R. "Housman's 'Farewell to Barn and Stack and Tree,' " *Explicator*, I (1942–43), Query 29.

Ransom, John Crowe. "Honey and Gall," *Southern Review*, VI (1940), 2–19.

Richards, Grant. *Housman 1897–1936*. New York: Oxford University Press, 1942.

Ricks, Christopher. "The Nature of Housman's Poetry," *Essays in Criticism*, XIV (1964), 268–84.

Robb, Nesca A. "A. E. Housman" in *Four in Exile*. London: Hutchinson, 1948, pp. 11–54.

Roberts, J. H. "Housman's 'Hell Gate,' " *Explicator*, V (1946–47), Item 44.

Robertson, D. S. "A. E. Housman," *Classical Review*, L (1936), 113–15.

Robinson, Oliver. *Angry Dust: The Poetry of A. E. Housman*. Boston: Humphries, 1950.

Rockwell, Kiffin Ayres. "A. E. Housman, Poet-Scholar," *Classical Journal*, LII (1957), 145–48.

Romana-Sastrin, V. V. "Professor Housman on Greek Astrology," *Classical Review*, XXXVI (1922), 20–21.

Ryan, John K. "Defeatist as Poet," *Catholic World*, CXLI (1935), 32–38.

Salinger, Herman. "Housman's *Last Poems*, XXX and Heine's *Lyrisches Intermezzo*, 62," *Modern Language Notes*, LIV (1939), 288–90.

Schneider, Elisabeth. *Aesthetic Motive.* New York: Macmillan, 1939.

Scott, Wilbur S. "Housman's 'Farewell to Barn and Stack and Tree,' " *Explicator,* V (1946–47), Item 11.

Scott-Craig, T.S.K. "Housman's '1887,' " *Explicator,* II (1943–44), Item 34.

Scott-Kilvert, Ian. *A. E. Housman.* London: Longmans, Green and Company, 1955.

Seigel, Jules Paul. "A. E. Housman's Modification of the Flower Motif of the Pastoral Elegy," *Victorian Poetry,* II (1964), 47–50.

Sitwell, Edith. "Three Eras of Modern Poetry" in *Trio* by Osbert, Edith, and Sacheverell Sitwell. London: Macmillan, 1938, pp. 97–139.

Sparrow, John. "Echoes in the Poetry of A. E. Housman," *Nineteenth Century,* CXV (1934), 243–56.

————. "A. E. Housman," *Spectator,* CLVI (May 8, 1936), 842.

————. "A. E. Housman's Poetry," *New Statesman and Nation,* XI (May 30, 1936), 855.

————. "G. A. Simcox, Mr. T. Burns Haber, and Housman's 'Hell Gate,' " *Philological Quarterly,* XXXIII (1954), 437–42.

————. "A Housman 'Reminiscence,' " *Review of English Studies,* X (1959), 183–85.

Spender, Stephen. "The Essential Housman" in *The Making of a Poem.* London: Harnish Hamilton, 1955, pp. 157–65.

Spivey, Edward. "Housman's 'The Oracles,' " *Explicator,* XXI (1962–63), Item 44.

Stallman, Robert W. "Annotated Bibliography of A. E. Housman: A Critical Study," PMLA, LX (1945), 463–502.

————. "Housman's 'On Wenlock Edge,' " *Explicator,* III (1944–45), Item 26.

Strozier, Robert I. "A. E. Housman: Image, Illogic and Allusion," *Colby Library Quarterly,* VII (1966), 257–63.

Stevenson, John W. "The Pastoral Setting in the Poetry of A. E. Housman," *South Atlantic Quarterly,* LV (1956), 487–500.

————. "The Martyr as Innocent: Housman's Lonely Lad," *South Atlantic Quarterly*, LVII (1958), 69–85.

————. "Housman's Lyric Tradition," *Forum*, IV (1962), 17–21.

Sullivan, Frank. "Housman's 'Farewell to Barn and Stack and Tree,' " *Explicator*, II (1943–44), Item 36.

Symons, Katherine E., et al. *Alfred Edward Housman: Recollections*. New York: Holt, 1937.

Taylor, George A. "A. E. Housman," *Queen's Quarterly*, XLIII (1936–37), 383–90.

Untermeyer, Louis. "A. E. Housman" in *Modern American Poetry; Modern British Poetry*. New York: Harcourt, Brace, 1942, II, 101–103.

Van Doren, Carl, and Mark Van Doren. *American and British Literature Since 1890*. New York: Century, 1925.

Walcutt, Charles C. "Housman's '1887,' " *Explicator*, II (1943–44), Item 34.

Walton, Eda Lou. "Not Mine, But Man's," *Nation*, CXLIII (November 7, 1936), 552.

Watson, George L. *A. E. Housman: A Divided Life*. London: Rupert Hart-Davis, 1957.

Werner, W. L. "Housman's '1887'—No Satire," *College English*, VI (1944), 165–66.

————. "Housman's 'Loveliest of Trees,' " *Explicator*, V (1946–47), Item 4.

————. "Housman's 'Terence, This Is Stupid Stuff,' " *Explicator*, XIV (1955–56), Item 2.

White, William. "Two Problems in A. E. Housman Bibliography," *Papers of the Bibliographical Society of America*, XLV (1951), 358–59.

————. " 'The Death of Socrates': A. E. Housman's First Published Poem," *PMLA*, LXVIII (1953), 913–16.

————. "A. E. Housman Anthologized: Evidence in the Growth of a Poet's Reputation," *Bulletin of Bibliography*, XXI (1953), 43–48, 68–72.

————. "*A Shropshire Lad* in Progress," *The Library*, IX (1954), 255–64.

————. "A Missing Comma in A. E. Housman," *American Notes and Queries*, V (1966), 22–23.

Whitridge, Arnold. "Vigny and Housman: A Study in Pessimism," *American Scholar*, X (1941), 156–69.

Wilbur, Richard. "Round About a Poem of Housman's" in *The Moment of Poetry*, ed. by Don Cameron Allen. Baltimore: Johns Hopkins Press, 1962, pp. 73–98.

Williams, Harold. *Modern English Writers*. London: Sidgwick and Jackson, 1925.

Wilson, Edmund. "A. E. Housman" in *The Triple Thinkers*. New York: Oxford University Press, 1948, pp. 60–71.

Withers, Percy. *A Buried Life*. London: Jonathan Cape, 1940.

Wysong, J. N. "A. E. Housman's Use of Astronomy," *Anglia*, LXXX (1962), 295–301.

Zabel, Morton D. "The Intimate Stranger," *New Republic*, CVI (April 13, 1942), 510–12.

————. "The Whole of Housman," *Nation*, CL (June 1, 1940), 684–86.

INDEX